# RZLBD LETTERS

# RZLBD LETTERS

Reza Aliabadi **(RZLBD)**

Rochester
New York

**RIT** | **RIT Press**

Published and distributed by:
RIT Press
90 Lomb Memorial Drive
Rochester, New York 14623
https://press.rit.edu

Printed in the United States of America

ISBN 978-1-956313-23-9 (print)


Library of Congress Cataloging-in-Publication Data

Names: Aliabadi, Reza, author.
Title: RZLBD letters / Reza Aliabadi (RZLBD).
Other titles: RZLBD letters. Selections
Description: Rochester, New York : RIT Press, [2024]
Identifiers: LCCN 2024039389 | ISBN 9781956313239 (paperback)
Subjects: LCSH: Aliabadi, Reza—Themes, motives. | Typewriter art—
    Canada—Themes, motives.
Classification: LCC N6549.A535 A74 2024 | DDC 700/.457—dc23/
    eng/20240901
LC record available at https://lccn.loc.gov/2024039389

We gather on the traditional territory of the Onöndowa'ga:' or "the
people of the Great Hill." In English, they are known as Seneca people,
"the keeper of the western door." They are one of the six nations that
make up the sovereign Haudenosaunee Confederacy.

We honor the land on which RIT was built and recognize the unique
relationship that the Indigenous stewards have with this land. That
relationship is the core of their traditions, cultures, and histories. We
recognize the history of genocide, colonization, and assimilation
of Indigenous people that took place on this land. Mindful of these
histories, we work towards understanding, acknowledging, and
ultimately reconciliation.


Cover image: Self portrait, courtesy of Atelier RZLBD.

*Words are the source of misunderstandings.*
—
Antoine de Saint-Exupery

# CONTENTS

# FOREWORD

# ANALOGOUS HAPTICS

*The inferno of the living is not something that will be; if there is one, it is what is already here, the inferno where we live every day, that we form by being together.*
—

Italo Calvino

People who share a common vision or outlook on the world are few and far between.

There is something about the analog world that appeals deeply to people like Reza Aliabadi and me. The subtle, audible crackle of a record as a finger gently guides the needle into its groove; the whirring click of a rotary-phone dial in anticipation of a remote human voice connection; the positive click of a shift into first gear as an automobile engages, lunging forward as if by physical command: these represent analog haptics of a certain age when the fidelity of precision tools were closely guided by the human hand — experiences missing from many of today's analogous, banal acts of life. Our shared interest in analog haptics is driven by more than nostalgia — it is a fundamental attitude that seeks to connect with a certain cultural production, often associated with the output of modernism.

*You can reach timelessness if you look for the essence of things and not the appearance.*
—

Massimo Vignelli

I often say that "all roads lead to the Vignelli Center." And while I tend to accompany this remark with a wink, it is certainly true for my journey. The Vignelli Center for Design Studies played a significant role in attracting me to the Rochester Institute of Technology (RIT) during the year of its construction, and currently it keeps me engaged in my activities there. Reza Aliabadi is a fellow traveler whose path also drew him to the center because of his passion for the particular approach to modernism left in their archives by the Vignellis. So, it could be said that Lella and Massimo Vignelli set the stage for this friendship and for the corresponding output it would engender.

*I like ruins because what remains is not the total design, but the clarity of thought, the naked structure, the spirit of the thing.*
—

Tadao Ando

Like a stonecutter, Reza Aliabadi has slowly and deliberately pressed the tools of his devotion into the pages of this book with both love and urgency. The addressees of his enclosed letters are his heroes and his friends because he has studied them. The impressions each has left on the world are enduring symbols of an architecture of both form and meaning dear to him. Some he has befriended; others he has never met. Alive or dead, known or unmet, the typed words and symbols pledge a visceral allegiance to the lessons he has absorbed as semiotic ontologies. Aliabadi's letters are monastic ritual. They are manifestations of devotion. They are purposefully indelible marks, offerings to Aliabadi's own gods.

2

*Some people cannot see a good thing when it is right here, right now. Others can sense a good thing coming when it is days, months, or miles away.*
—

Maya Angelou

My dear friend Reza Aliabadi stands with one foot firmly planted in the past and one extended into the future. This posture shows that his practice continues to evolve, built upon the shoulders of his giants. This same gesture and corresponding understanding adds richness to his work and to the value of this book, giving it agency — the recipe for its genius and for his.

Josh Owen
President, Josh Owen LLC
Vignelli Distinguished Professor of Design and Director of the
Vignelli Center for Design Studies at RIT

**PREFACE**

# SHINING WORDS

*Words are shining paragons of the loveliness of language.*
—
Emmett Williams

I am well aware of the work of Atelier RZLBD and the architecture and versatility of Aliabadi's formal design sensibilities, and what a delight it is to learn about and view *RZLBD Letters*. It follows so well his stated goal of exploring what he calls "at any level of design the adherence to a set of rules that allow a formal concept to be more present and integrated throughout."

Letterform is one of the most basic elements in a designer's toolbox. The graphic expressions of the design boom carry me back to an earlier interest in concrete poetry. This creative expression is an arrangement of linguistic elements in which the typographical effect is more important in conveying meaning than verbal significance. It is sometimes referred to as visual poetry, a term that has now developed a distinct meaning of its own. Understood in simpler terms, concrete poetry is a kind of linguistic art in which the way words and letters look is as important as what they mean. Today, concrete poetry is perhaps unique among avant-garde literary movements in being more popular outside academic institutions than within them, and it is ironically better known than the movement that inspired it: concrete art.

The multifarious expressions of these typographic compositions emphasize nonlinguistic elements in meaning in that the typeface creates a visual image for the person. I compliment Reza on this graphic quest for *RZLBD Letters*, and I hearten him onward to future creative journeys.

R. Roger Remington
Vignelli Distinguished Professor of Design Emeritus

# INTRODUCTION

# RZLBD LETTERS

With the invasion of digital media — the abundance of all sorts of smart gadgets at our disposal, and the fashionable trend of texting, iMessaging, FaceTiming, Zooming, and many more — taking the time to write a letter on a piece of paper has become obsolete, or at least a forgotten craft! Even more so if that letter has been typed with a manual typewriter. To take it one step further, this may also seem like an unusual idea if that letter is written to someone who has passed away or who is out of our reach! Odd maybe, but of course, this is not new. Indeed, the idea has been around for a long time and for many reasons, mostly to deal with grief, to pay an overdue respect, to make a confession, to secretly declare love and affection, and the like.

In my case, during the spring of 2020, after I got my hands on a vintage manual typewriter — an Olivetti Valentine portable machine — I decided to pay homage to a group of artists who have inspired me deeply. With a degree of madness, I started typing to them, in a language that on the surface may seem familiar to everyone, yet only each artist can fully decipher their particular letter.

*RZLBD Letters* is an ongoing project exploring the capacity of the letter as a medium and the manual typewriter as an instrument beyond their common or utilitarian purpose. Call this a romantic love affair or a nostalgic scribble — these correspondences allow me to spend extra time with and delve deeper into the visual domains of these brilliant creatives. Pursuing the letters in serial format articulates a body of work that offers many readings.

RZLBD (Reza Aliabadi)
Founder & Principal, Atelier RZLBD
Vignelli Center Inaugural Designer in Residence

```
1 1 1 1 1 1 2 2 2 2 2 2 3 3 3 3 3 3
1 1 1 1 1 1 2 2 2 2 2 2 3 3 3 3 3 3
1 1 1 1 1 1 2 2 2 2 2 2 3 3 3 3 3 3
1 1 1 1 1 1 2 2 2 2 2 2 3 3 3 3 3 3
1 1 1 1 1 1 2 2 2 2 2 2 3 3 3 3 3 3
1 1 1 1 1 1 2 2 2 2 2 2 3 3 3 3 3 3
4 4 4 4 4 4 5 5 5 5 5 5 6 6 6 6 6 6
4 4 4 4 4 4 5 5 5 5 5 5 6 6 6 6 6 6
4 4 4 4 4 4 5 5 5 5 5 5 6 6 6 6 6 6
4 4 4 4 4 4 5 5 5 5 5 5 6 6 6 6 6 6
4 4 4 4 4 4 5 5 5 5 5 5 6 6 6 6 6 6
4 4 4 4 4 4 5 5 5 5 5 5 6 6 6 6 6 6
7 7 7 7 7 7 8 8 8 8 8 8 9 9 9 9 9 9
7 7 7 7 7 7 8 8 8 8 8 8 9 9 9 9 9 9
7 7 7 7 7 7 8 8 8 8 8 8 9 9 9 9 9 9
7 7 7 7 7 7 8 8 8 8 8 8 9 9 9 9 9 9
7 7 7 7 7 7 8 8 8 8 8 8 9 9 9 9 9 9
7 7 7 7 7 7 8 8 8 8 8 8 9 9 9 9 9 9
```

To Carl Andre
Untitled 1960
11 May 2020

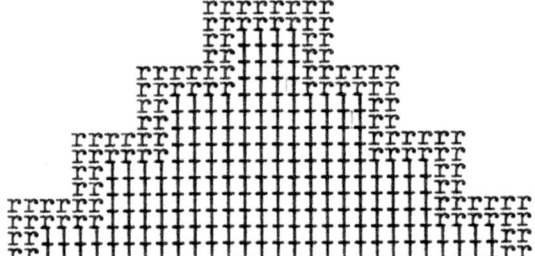

To Richard Long
Southern Gravity 2011
11 May 2020

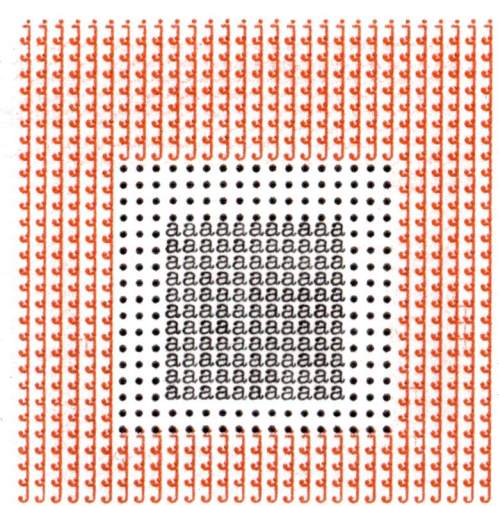

To Josef Albers
Tap Root 1965
11 May 2020

```
pppppppm
pppppppm
pppppppm
pppppppm
pppppppm
pppppppm
pppppppm
pppppppm
pppppppm
pppppppm
mmmmmmmm
mmmmmmmm
        m
        m
        m
        m
        m
        m
mmmmmmmmmmmmmmmmmmmmmmmmmmmmmmmmmm
        m                    mcccc
        m                    mcccc
        m                    mcccc
        m                    mcccc
        m                    mcccc
        m                    m
        m                    m
        m                    m
        m                    m
```

To Piet Mondrian
Composition (No. 1) with Red & Black 1929
12 May 2020

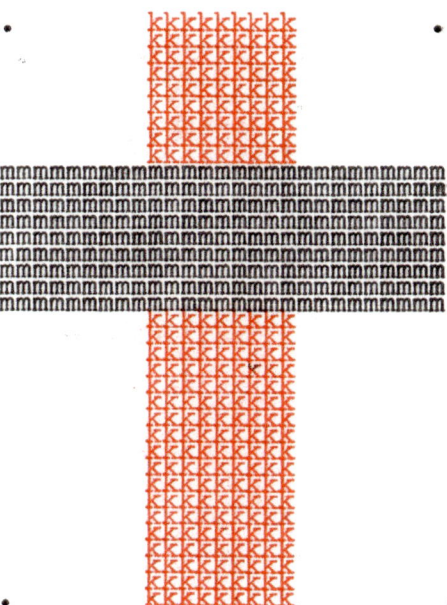

To Kazimir Malevich
Supermatist Cross 1920
12 May 2020

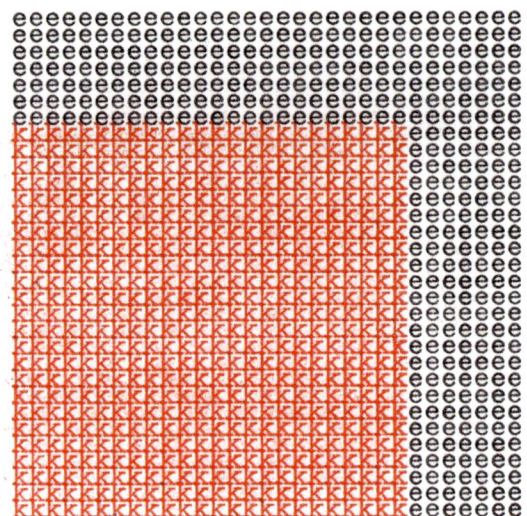

To Ellsworth Kelly
Red on Black 2001
12 May 2020

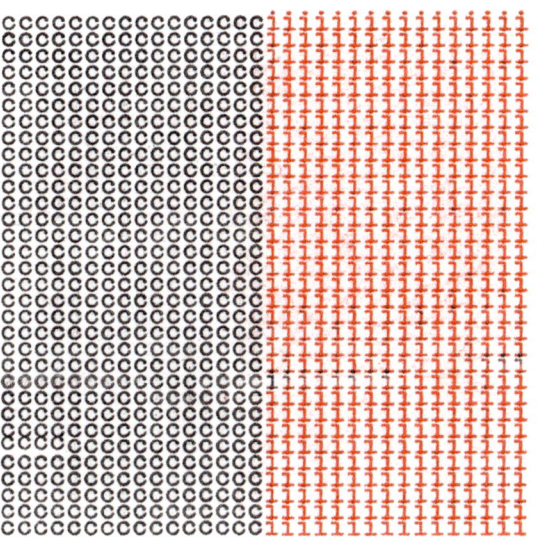

To Callum Innes
Untitled Lamp Black No. 7 2014
13 May 2020

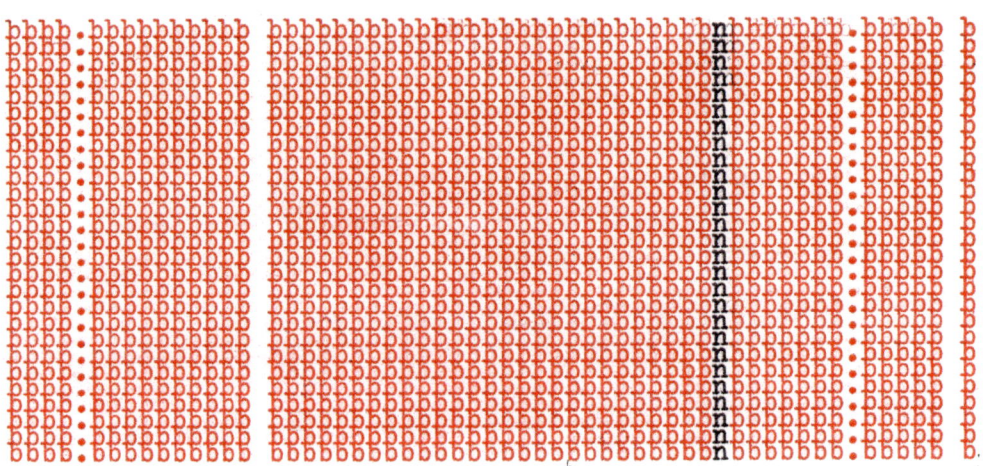

To Barnett Newman
Vir Heroicus Sublimis 1950–51
13 May 2020

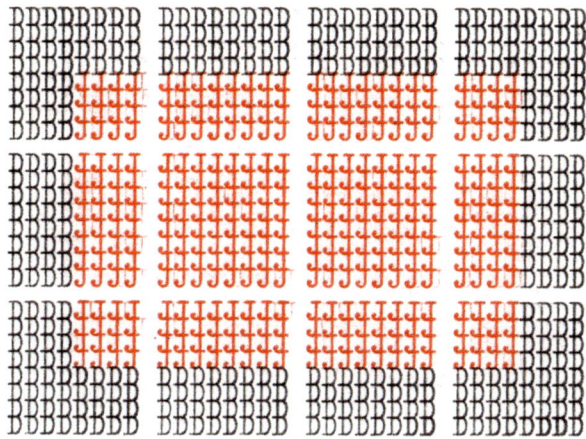

To Donald Judd
Untitled S. 295 1993
13 May 2020

To Frank Stella
The Marriage of Reason & Squalor II 1959
14 May 2020

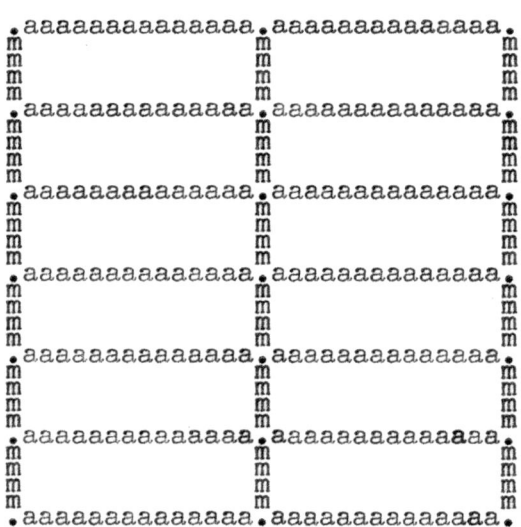

To Agnes Martin
On a Clear Day 1973
14 May 2020

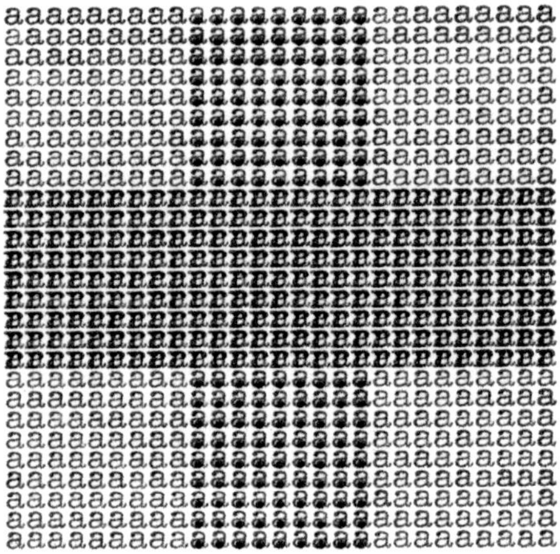

To Ad Reinhardt
Ultimate Painting No. 5 1962
14 May 2020

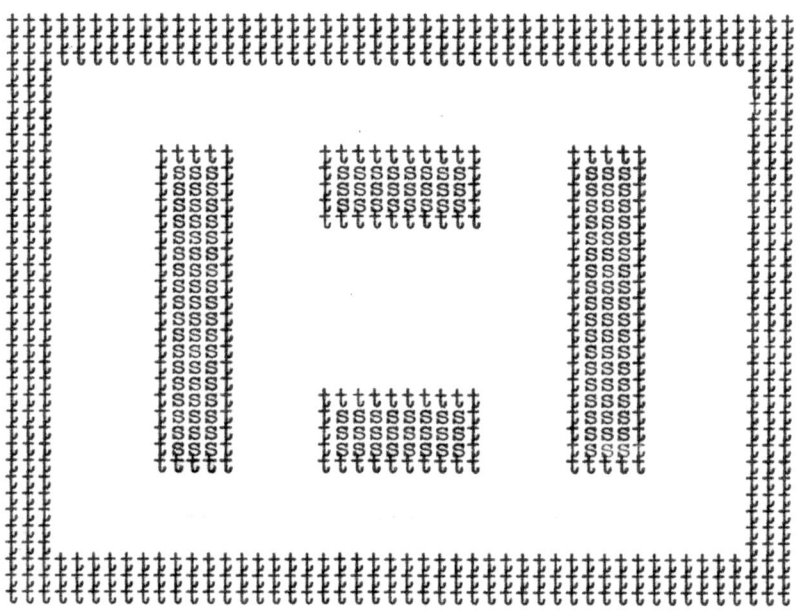

To Tony Smith
Untitled (Drawing of Maze) 1967
14 May 2020

25 Letters To <u>Agnes Martin</u>
16,640 x
05 - 09 May 2020

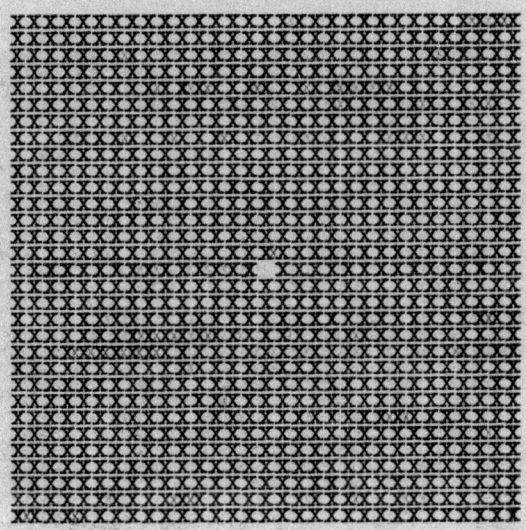

01/25 (1x1)
960 x
05 May 2020

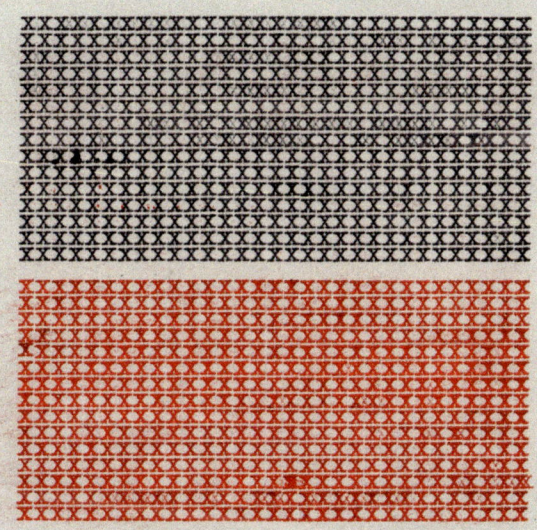

02/25 (1x2)
930 x
05 May 2020

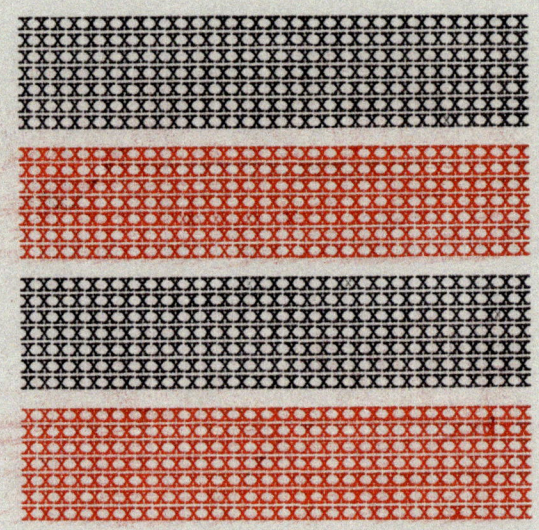

03/25 (1x4)
868 x
05 May 2020

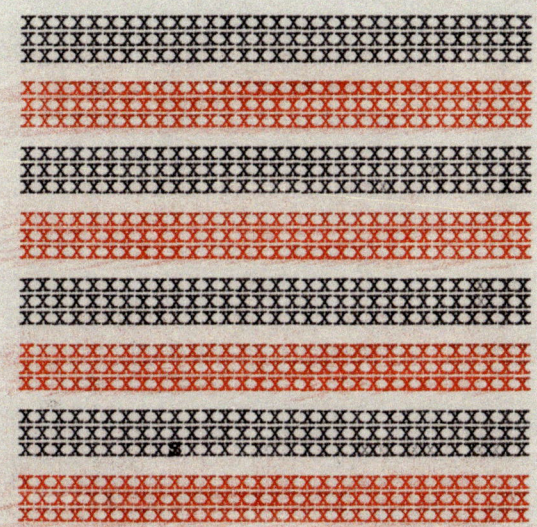

04/25 ((1x8)
744 x
05 May 2020)

```
XXXXXXXXXXXXXXXXXXXXXXXXXXXXXXXXXX
XXXXXXXXXXXXXXXXXXXXXXXXXXXXXXXXXX
XXXXXXXXXXXXXXXXXXXXXXXXXXXXXXXXXX
XXXXXXXXXXXXXXXXXXXXXXXXXXXXXXXXXX
XXXXXXXXXXXXXXXXXXXXXXXXXXXXXXXXXX
XXXXXXXXXXXXXXXXXXXXXXXXXXXXXXXXXX
XXXXXXXXXXXXXXXXXXXXXXXXXXXXXXXXXX
XXXXXXXXXXXXXXXXXXXXXXXXXXXXXXXXXX
XXXXXXXXXXXXXXXXXXXXXXXXXXXXXXXXXX
XXXXXXXXXXXXXXXXXXXXXXXXXXXXXXXXXX
XXXXXXXXXXXXXXXXXXXXXXXXXXXXXXXXXX
XXXXXXXXXXXXXXXXXXXXXXXXXXXXXXXXXX
XXXXXXXXXXXXXXXXXXXXXXXXXXXXXXXXXX
XXXXXXXXXXXXXXXXXXXXXXXXXXXXXXXXXX
XXXXXXXXXXXXXXXXXXXXXXXXXXXXXXXXXX
XXXXXXXXXXXXXXXXXXXXXXXXXXXXXXXXXX
```

05/25 (1x16)
496 x
05 May 2020

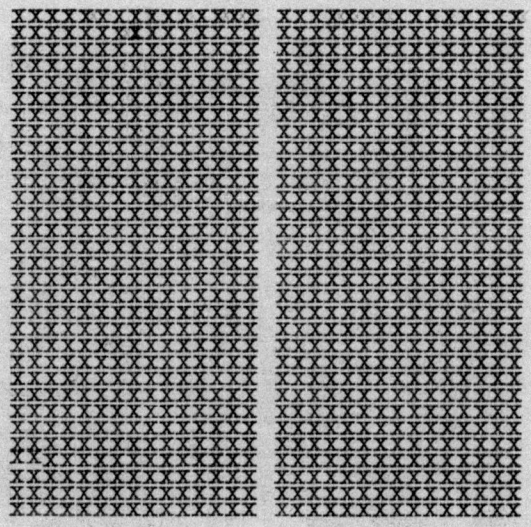

06/25 (2x1)
930 x
06 May 2020

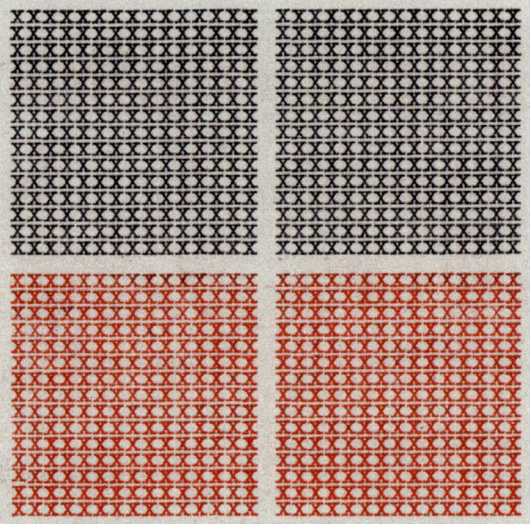

07/25 (2x2)
900 x
06 May 2020

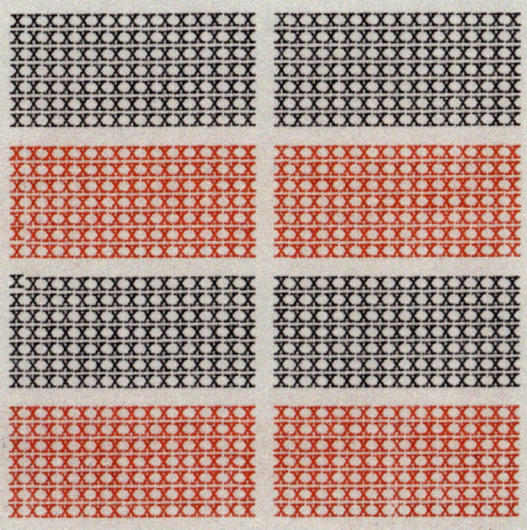

08/25 (2x4)
840 x
06 May 2020

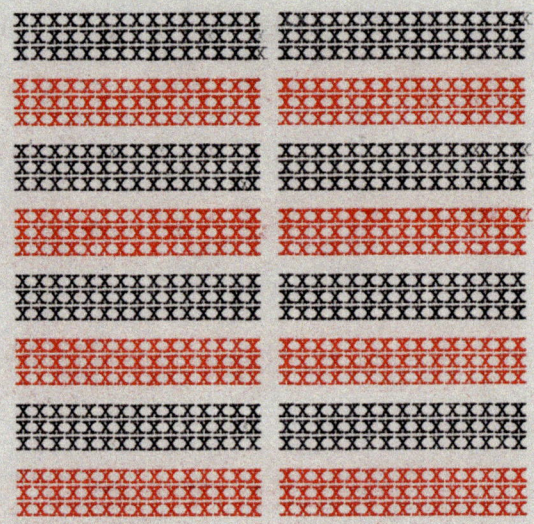

09/25 (2x8)
720 x
06 May 2020

XXXXXXXXXXXXXXXX XXXXXXXXXXXXXXXX
XXXXXXXXXXXXXXXX XXXXXXXXXXXXXXXX
XXXXXXXXXXXXXXXX XXXXXXXXXXXXXXXX
XXXXXXXXXXXXXXXX XXXXXXXXXXXXXXXX
XXXXXXXXXXXXXXXX XXXXXXXXXXXXXXXX
XXXXXXXXXXXXXXXX XXXXXXXXXXXXXXXX
XXXXXXXXXXXXXXXX XXXXXXXXXXXXXXXX
XXXXXXXXXXXXXXXX XXXXXXXXXXXXXXXX
XXXXXXXXXXXXXXXX XXXXXXXXXXXXXXXX
XXXXXXXXXXXXXXXX XXXXXXXXXXXXXXXX
XXXXXXXXXXXXXXXX XXXXXXXXXXXXXXXX
XXXXXXXXXXXXXXXX XXXXXXXXXXXXXXXX
XXXXXXXXXXXXXXXX XXXXXXXXXXXXXXXX
XXXXXXXXXXXXXXXX XXXXXXXXXXXXXXXX
XXXXXXXXXXXXXXXX XXXXXXXXXXXXXXXX

10/25 (2x16)
480 x
06 May 2020

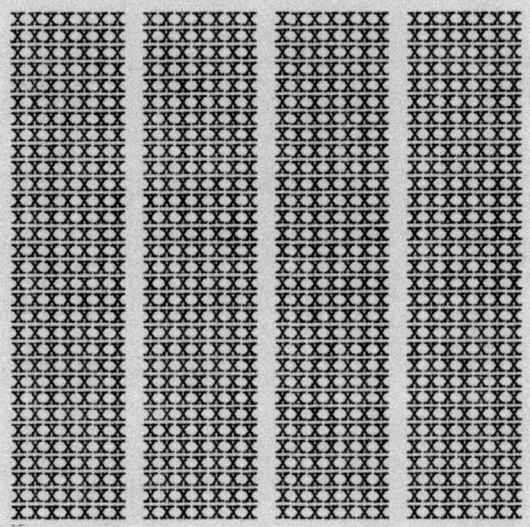

11/25 (4x1)
868 x
07 May 2020

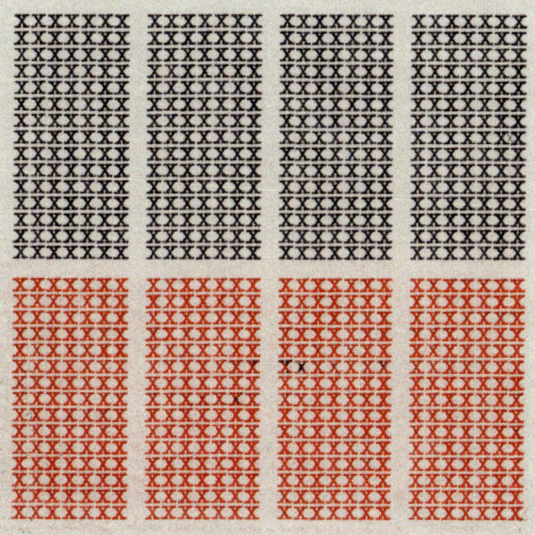

12/25 (4x2)
840 x
07 May 2020

13/25 (4x4)
784 x
07 May 2020

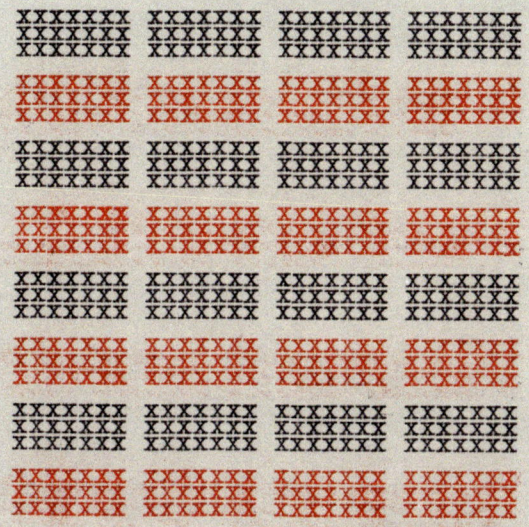

14/25 (4x8)
672 x
07 May 2020

```
XXXXXXX XXXXXXX XXXXXXX XXXXXXX
XXXXXXX XXXXXXX XXXXXXX XXXXXXX
XXXXXXX XXXXXXX XXXXXXX XXXXXXX
XXXXXXX XXXXXXX XXXXXXX XXXXXXX
XXXXXXX XXXXXXX XXXXXXX XXXXXXX
XXXXXXX XXXXXXX XXXXXXX XXXXXXX
XXXXXXX XXXXXXX XXXXXXX XXXXXXX
XXXXXXX XXXXXXX XXXXXXX XXXXXXX
XXXXXXX XXXXXXX XXXXXXX XXXXXXX
XXXXXXX XXXXXXX XXXXXXX XXXXXXX
XXXXXXX XXXXXXX XXXXXXX XXXXXXX
XXXXXXX XXXXXXX XXXXXXX XXXXXXX
XXXXXXX XXXXXXX XXXXXXX XXXXXXX
XXXXXXX XXXXXXX XXXXXXX XXXXXXX
XXXXXXX XXXXXXX XXXXXXX XXXXXXX
XXXXXXX XXXXXXX XXXXXXX XXXXXXX
```

15/25 (4x16)
448 x
07 May 2020

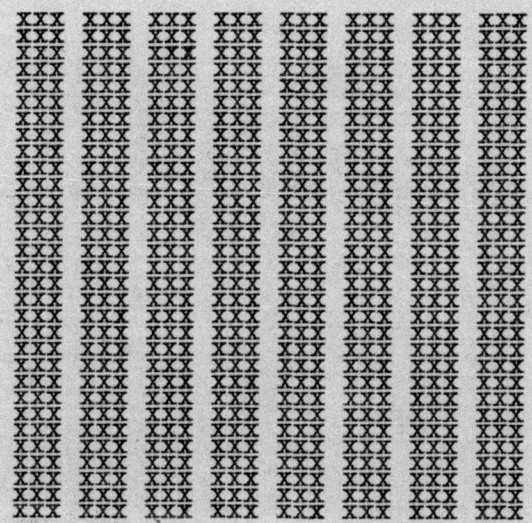

16/25 (8x1)
744 x
08 May 2020

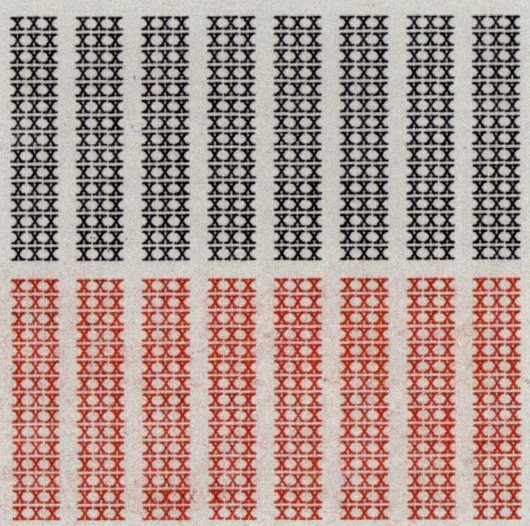

17/25 (8x2)
720 x
08 May 2020

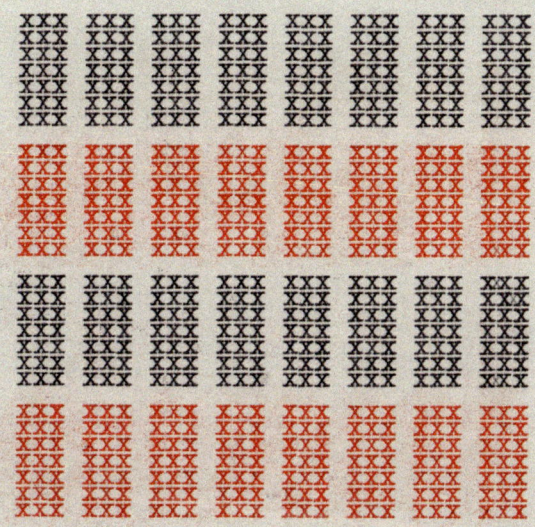

18/25 (8x4)
672 x
08 May 2020

19/25 (8x8)
576 x
08 May 2020

```
xxx xxx xxx xxx xxx xxx xxx xxx
xxx xxx xxx xxx xxx xxx xxx xxx
xxx xxx xxx xxx xxx xxx xxx xxx
xxx xxx xxx xxx xxx xxx xxx xxx
xxx xxx xxx xxx xxx xxx xxx xxx
xxx xxx xxx xxx xxx xxx xxx xxx
xxx xxx xxx xxx xxx xxx xxx xxx
xxx xxx xxx xxx xxx xxx xxx xxx
xxx xxx xxx xxx xxx xxx xxx xxx
xxx xxx xxx xxx xxx xxx xxx xxx
xxx xxx xxx xxx xxx xxx xxx xxx
xxx xxx xxx xxx xxx xxx xxx xxx
xxx xxx xxx xxx xxx xxx xxx xxx
xxx xxx xxx xxx xxx xxx xxx xxx
xxx xxx xxx xxx xxx xxx xxx xxx
xxx xxx xxx xxx xxx xxx xxx xxx
```

20/25 (8x16)
384 x
08 May 2020

21/25 (16x1)
496 x
09 May 2020

22/25 (16x2))
480 x
09 May 2020

XXXXXXXXXXXXXXXX
XXXXXXXXXXXXXXXX
XXXXXXXXXXXXXXXX
XXXXXXXXXXXXXXXX

XXXXXXXXXXXXXXXX
XXXXXXXXXXXXXXXX
XXXXXXXXXXXXXXXX
XXXXXXXXXXXXXXXX

XXXXXXXXXXXXXXXX
XXXXXXXXXXXXXXXX
XXXXXXXXXXXXXXXX
XXXXXXXXXXXXXXXX

XXXXXXXXXXXXXXXX
XXXXXXXXXXXXXXXX
XXXXXXXXXXXXXXXX
XXXXXXXXXXXXXXXX

23/25 (16x4)
448 x
09 May 2020

46

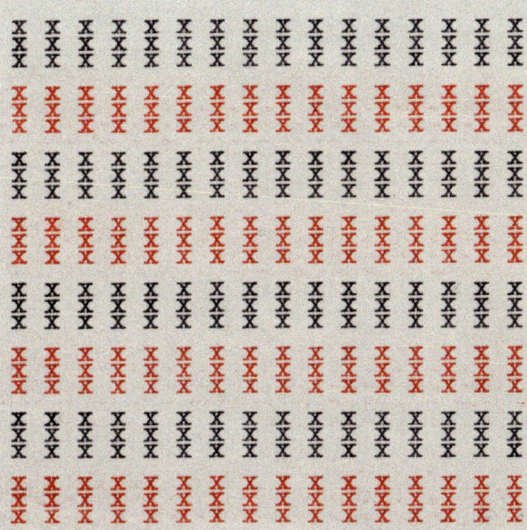

24/25 (16x8)
384 x
09 May 2020

```
X X X X X X X X X X X X X X X X
X X X X X X X X X X X X X X X X
X X X X X X X X X X X X X X X X
X X X X X X X X X X X X X X X X
X X X X X X X X X X X X X X X X
X X X X X X X X X X X X X X X X
X X X X X X X X X X X X X X X X
X X X X X X X X X X X X X X X X
X X X X X X X X X X X X X X X X
X X X X X X X X X X X X X X X X
X X X X X X X X X X X X X X X X
X X X X X X X X X X X X X X X X
X X X X X X X X X X X X X X X X
X X X X X X X X X X X X X X X X
X X X X X X X X X X X X X X X X
X X X X X X X X X X X X X X X X
```

25/25 (16x16)
256 x
09 May 2020

| 1x1 | 2x1 | 4x1 | 8x1 | 16x1 |
|-----|-----|-----|-----|------|
| 960 | 930 | 868 | 744 | 496  |

| 1x2 | 2x2 | 4x2 | 8x2 | 16x2 |
|-----|-----|-----|-----|------|
| 930 | 900 | 840 | 720 | 480  |

| 1x4 | 2x4 | 4x4 | 8x4 | 16x4 |
|-----|-----|-----|-----|------|
| 868 | 840 | 784 | 672 | 448  |

| 1x8 | 2x8 | 4x8 | 8x8 | 16x8 |
|-----|-----|-----|-----|------|
| 744 | 720 | 672 | 576 | 384  |

| 1x16 | 2x16 | 4x16 | 8x16 | 16x16 |
|------|------|------|------|-------|
| 496  | 480  | 448  | 384  | 256   |

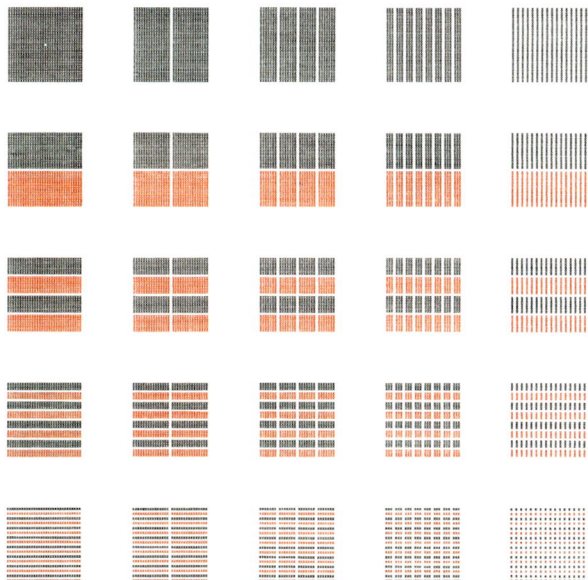

20 Letters To <u>Donald Judd</u>
3951 <u>D</u> + 3951 <u>J</u>
May 2020

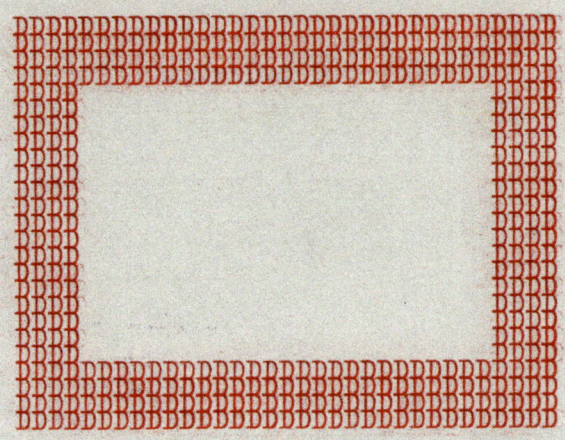

To Donald Judd
Untitled (Schellmann 157-166) 1/10
15 May 2020

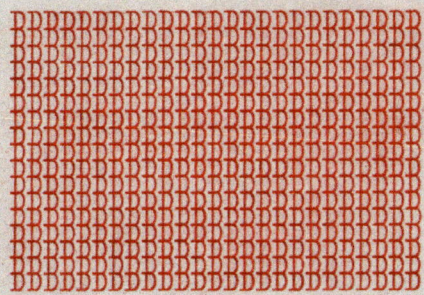

To Donald Judd
Untitled (Schellmann 157-166) 2/10
15 May 2020

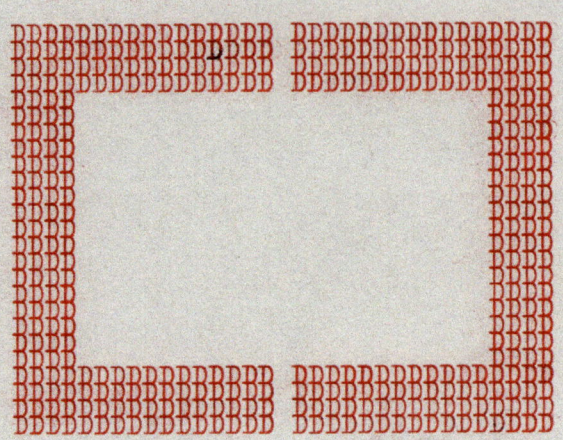

To Donald Judd

Untitled (Schellmann 157–166) 3/10
15 May 2020

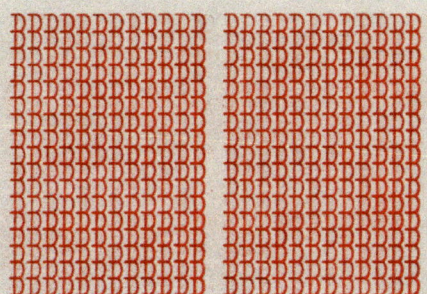

To Donald Judd
Untitled (Schellmann 157–166) 4/10
15 May 2020

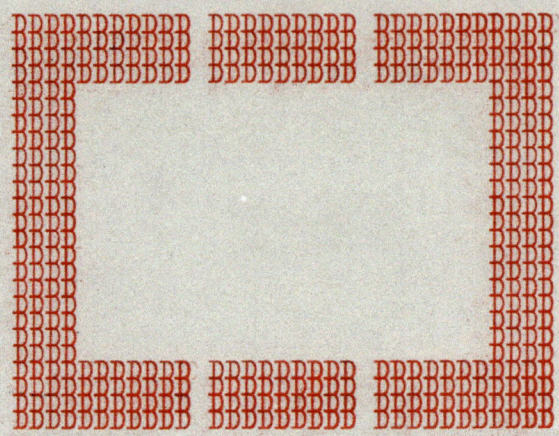

To Donald Judd
Untitled (Schellmann 157-166) 5/10
15 May 2020

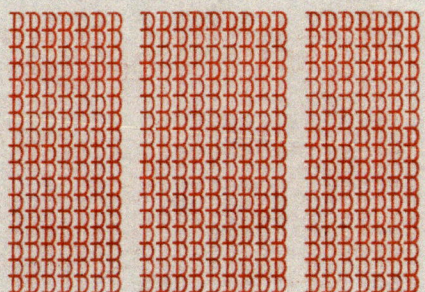

To Donald Judd
Untitled (Schellmann 157-166) 6/10
15 May 2020

To Donald Judd
Untitled (Schellman 157-166) 7/10
15 May 2020

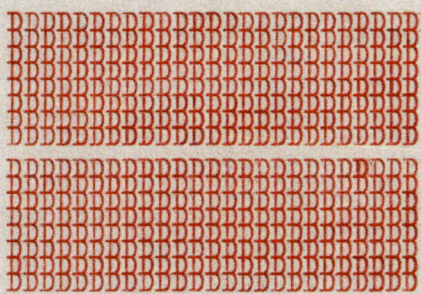

To Donald Judd
Untitled (Schellmann 157–166) 8/10
15 May 2020

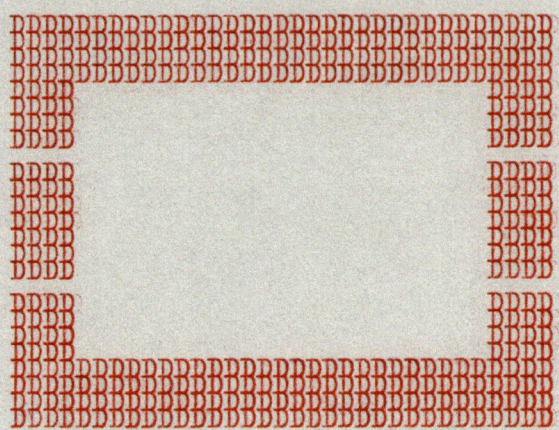

To Donald Judd
Untitled (Schellmann 157–166) 9/10
15 May 2020

62

To Donald Judd
Untitled (Schellmann 157-166) 10/10
15 May 2020

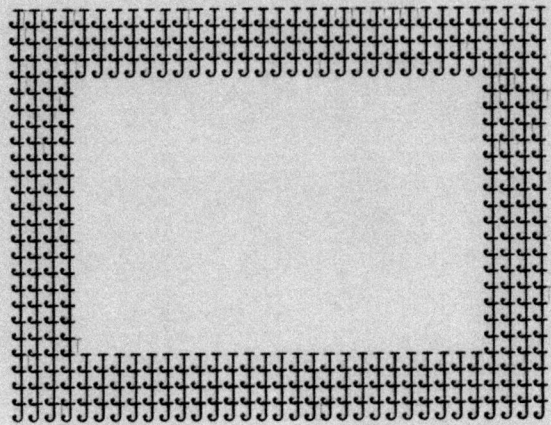

To Donald Judd
Untitled (Schellmann 177-186) 1/10
17 May 2020

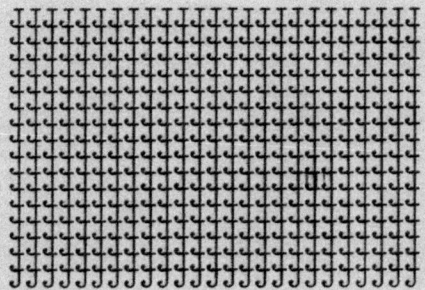

To Donald Judd
Untitled (Schellman 177–186) 2/10
17 May 2020

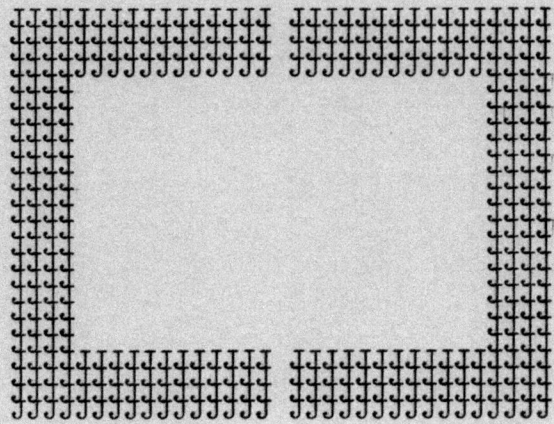

To Donald Judd
Untitled (Schellmann 177—186) 3/10
17 May 2020

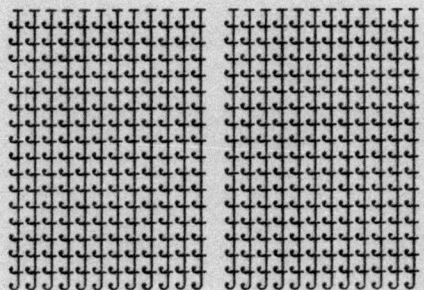

To Donald Judd
Untitled (Schellman 177-186) 4/10
17 May 2020

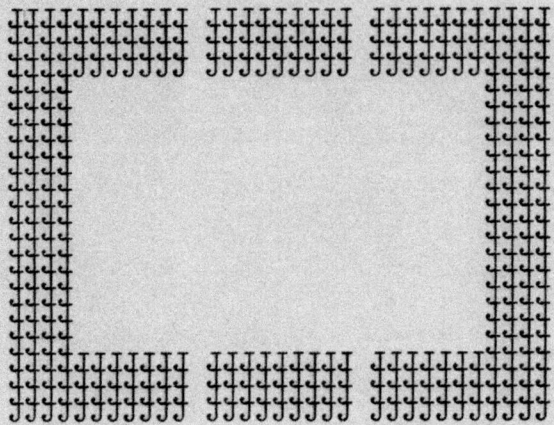

To Donald Judd
Untitled (Schellmann 177–186) 5/10
17 May 2020

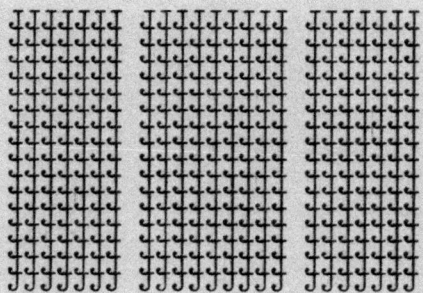

To Donald Judd
Untitled (Schellmann 177–186) 6/10
17 May 2020

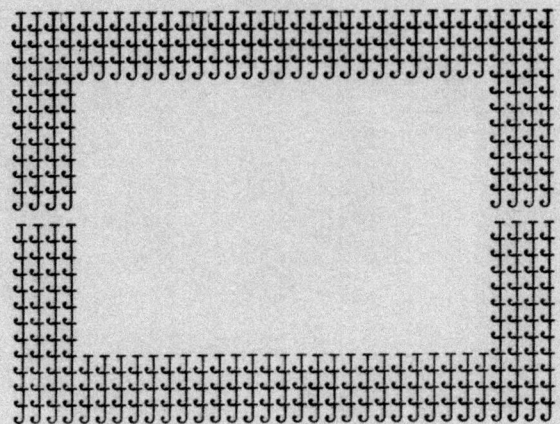

To Donald Judd
Untitled (Schellmann 177–186) 7/10
17 May 2020

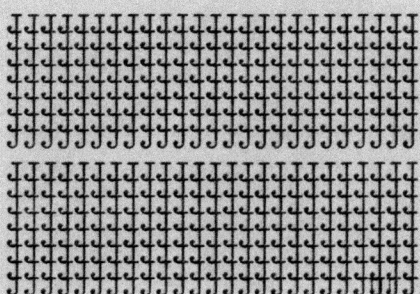

To Donald Judd
Untitled (Schellmann 177-186) 8/10
17 May 2020

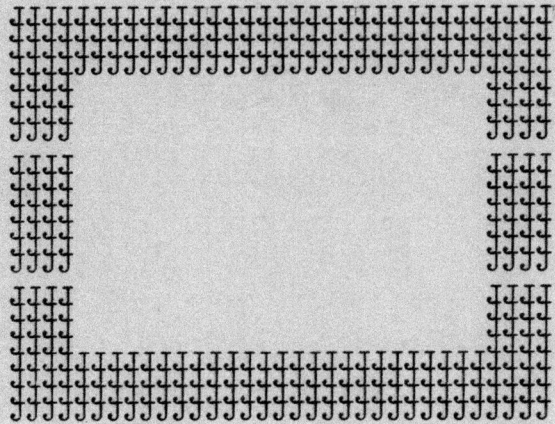

To Donald Judd
Untitled (Schellmann 177-186) 9/10
17 May 2020

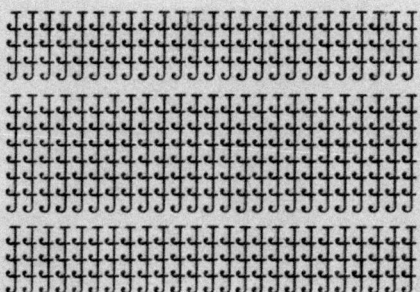

To Donald Judd
Untitled (Schellmann 177-186) 10/10
17 May 2020

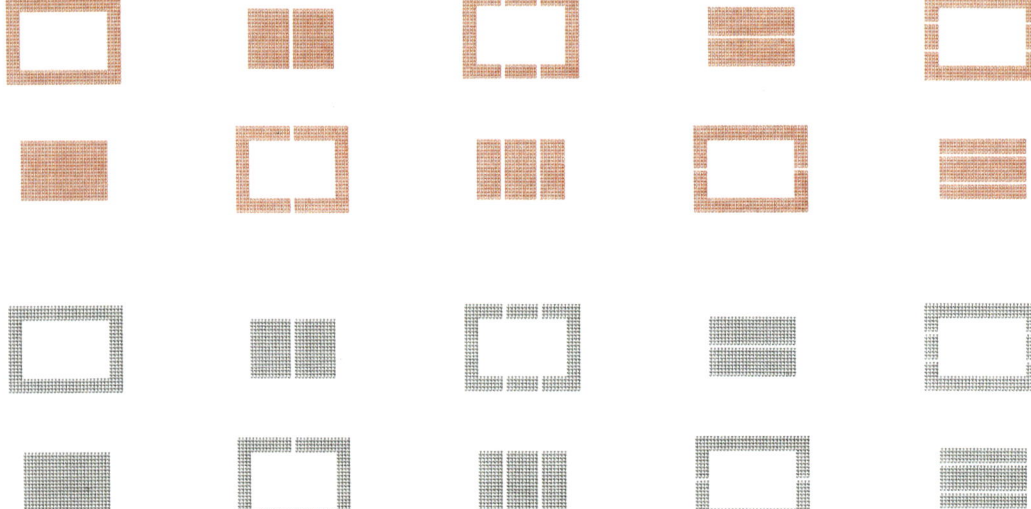

9 Letters To Frank Stella
Black Series I 1967
July 2020

To Frank Stella
Black Series I (1/9) 1967
10 July 2020

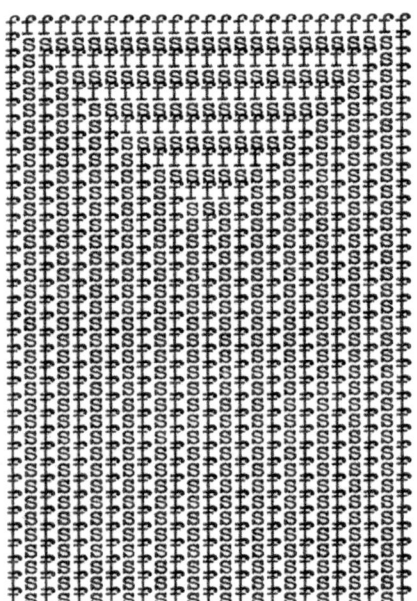

To Frank Stella  
Black Series I (2/9) 1967  
10 July 2020

```
fsfsfsfsfsfsfssfsfsfsfsfsf
fsfsfsfsfsfsssfsfsfsfsfsf
fsfsfsfsfsfsssfsfsfsfsfsf
fsfsfsfsfsfsssfsfsfsfsfsf
fsfsfsfsfsfsfssfsfsfsfsfsf
fsfsfsfsfsfsssfsfsfsfsfsf
fsfsfsfsfsfssssfsfsfsfsfsf
fsfsfsfsfsfssssssssfsfsfsf
fsfsfsfsfssssssssssfsfsfsf
fsfsfsfsfssssssssssssfsfsf
fsfsfsfstttttttttttttfsfsf
fsfsfsfstssssssssssssssfsf
fsfsfstttttttttttttttttsf
fsfssssssssssssssssssssssf
fsttttttttttttttttttttttf
SSSSSSSSSSSSSSSSSSSSSSSSS
SfttttttttttttttttttttfS
SfSssssssssssssssssssfS
SfSttttttttttttttttfSfS
SfSfStttttttttttfSfSfS
SfSfSfssssssssssfSfSfS
SfSfSfStttttttttSfSfSfS
SfSfSfStssssssssfSfSfS
SfSfSfSfStsssstSfSfSfS
SfSfSfSfSfSfSfSfSfSfSfS
SfSfSfSfSfSfSfSfSfSfSfS
SfSfSfSfSfSfSfSfSfSfSfS
SfSfSfSfSfSfSfSfSfSfSfS
SfSfSfSfSfSfSfSfSfSfSfS
SfSfSfSfSfSfSfSfSfSfSfS
SfSfSfSfSfSfSfSfSfSfSfS
```

To Frank Stella
Black Series I (3/9) 1967
10 July 2020

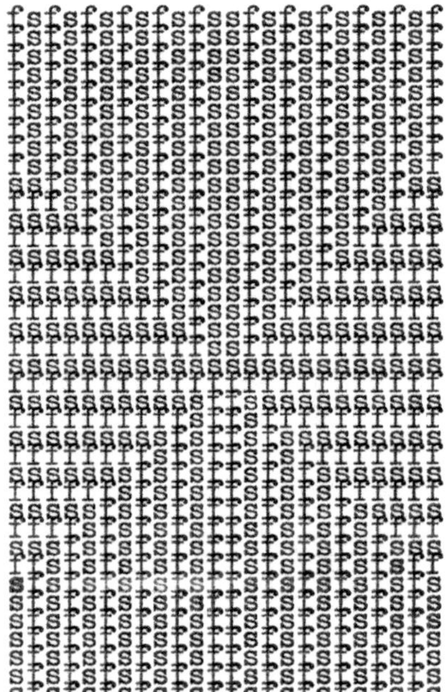

To Frank Stella
Black Series I (4/9) 1967
11 July 2020

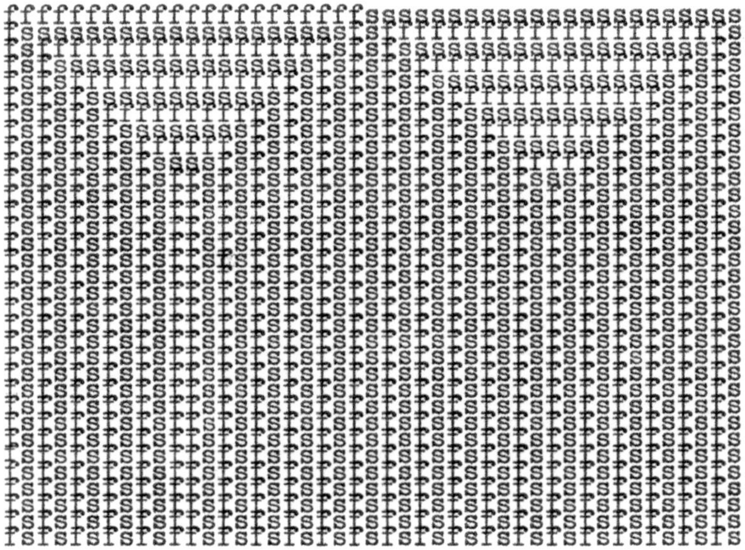

To Frank Stella
Black Series I (5/9) 1967
11 July 2020

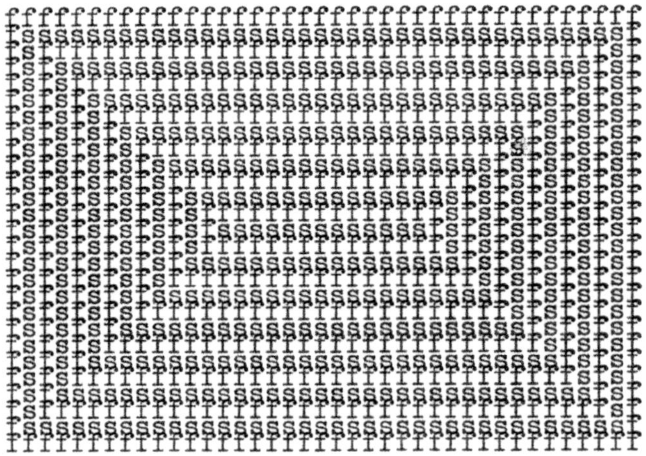

To Frank Stella
Black Series I (6/9) 1967
11 July 2020

```
fffffffffffffffffffffffffffffffff
fSSSSSSSSSSSSSSSSSSSSSSSSSSSSSSSSf
fSfIIIIIIIIIIIIIIIIIIIIIIIIIIIISf
fSfSSSSSSSSSSSSSSSSSSSSSSSSSSfSf
fSfSfIIIIIIIIIIIIIIIIIIIIIISfSf
fSfSfSSSSSSSSSSSSSSSSSSSSfSfSf
fSfSfSfIIIIIIIIIIIIIIIISfSfSf
fSfSfSfSSSSSSSSSSSSSSfSfSfSf
fSfSfSfSfIIIIIIIIIISfSfSfSf
fSfSfSfSfSSSSSSSSfSfSfSfSf
fSfSfSfSfSfIIIIIISfSfSfSfSf
fSfSfSfSfSfSSSSfSfSfSfSfSf
fSfSfSfSfSfSfSSfSfSfSfSfSf
fSfSfSfSfSfSfSSfSfSfSfSfSf
fSfSfSfSfSfSfSSfSfSfSfSfSf
fSfSfSfSfSfSfSSfSfSfSfSfSf
fSfSfSfSfSfSfSSfSfSfSfSfSf
fSfSfSfSfSfSfSSfSfSfSfSfSf
fSfSfSfSfSfSfSSfSfSfSfSfSf
fSfSfSfSfSfSfSSfSfSfSfSfSf
fSfSfSfSfSfSfSSfSfSfSfSfSf
fSfSfSfSfSfSfSfSSfSfSfSfSfSf
fSfSfSfSfSfSfSfSSfSfSfSfSfSf
```

To Frank Stella
Black Series I (7/9) 1967
12 July 2020

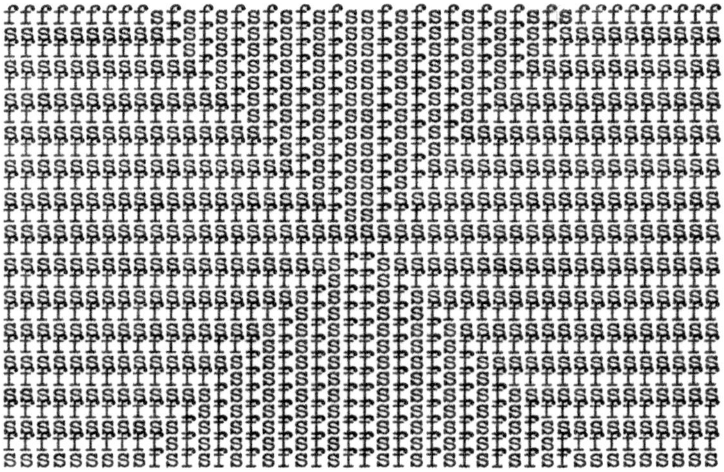

To Frank Stella
Black Series I (8/9) 1967
12 July 2020

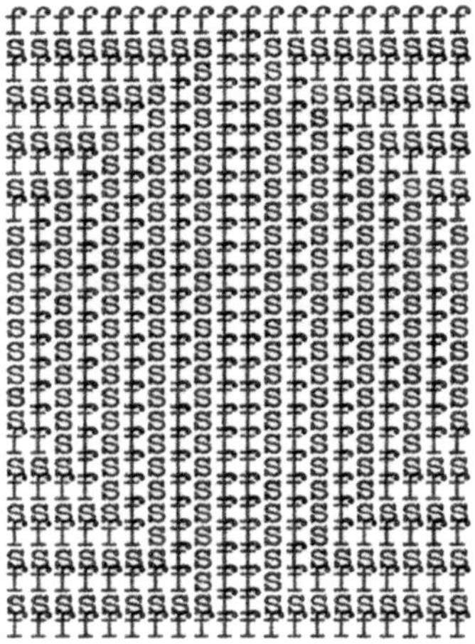

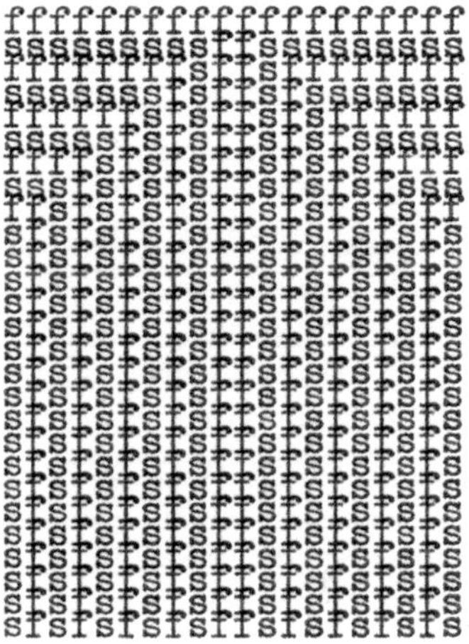

To Frank Stella
Black Series I (9/9) 1967
12 July 2020

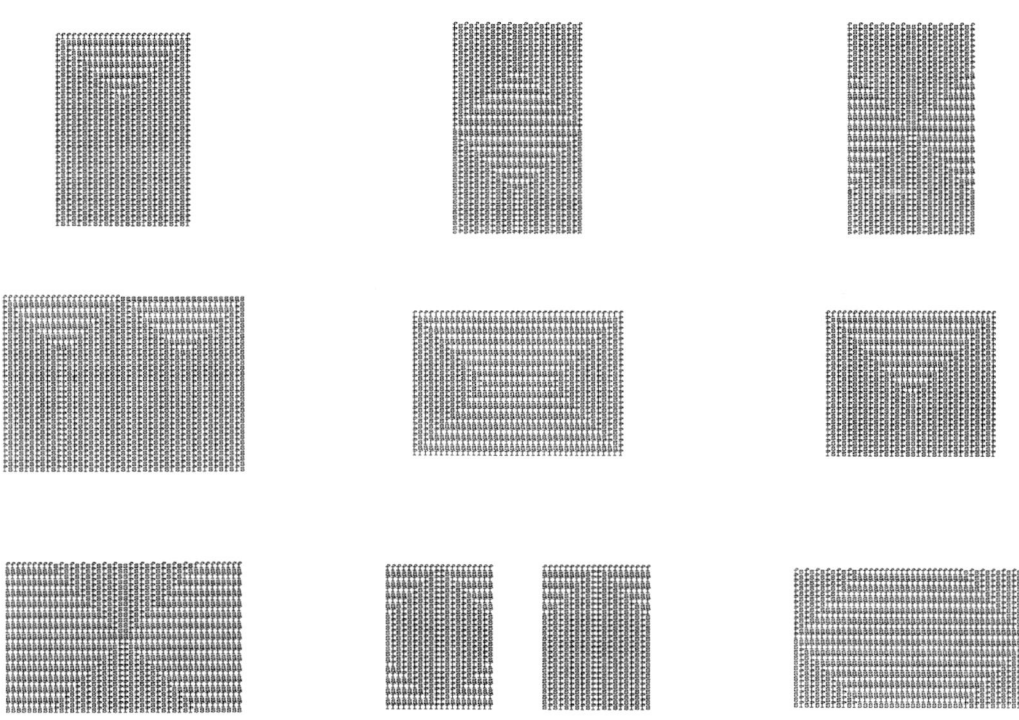

SPACE

The mind knows what the eye has not seen.
_ Agnes Martin

Long before we take the first breath in this planet or see the light of
our solar system, we had been confined in a womb. Before our conscious eyes
see any images in the vast universe (retinal, external form, exteriority)
our subconscious body feels the comfort within a small space surrounding it
(haptic, interior space, interiority).Maybe that is why from the very
moment we are born we are seeking for a shelter, for a refuge. For an
infant this could be the warm body of the mother, for a kid it comes as
hiding underneath a table, for a child it unfolds as the intimacy of a
small tent or a treehouse, until for an adult the necessity of dwelling
can be fulfilled in the spatial offerings of architecture.

My awe and wonder at this phenomenon makes me to believe that all the raw
materials that I need as an architect are contained in this analogy. Very
recently, Richard Serra's essay on Weight reminded me of Italo Calvino's
memo on Lightness, and both texts inspired me to make my own confession,
more or less in a similar way; in my case the obsession goes with Space.

Space is in essence that for which room has been made,
that which is let into its bounds.
_ Martin Heidegger

Space as the contained is a value very dear to me, not that it is any more
compelling than form as the container, but I am simply more fascinated
with the invisible vs. the visible, more captivated by the poetry of the
emptiness vs. the reality of the physical, more interested in the imagination
vs. the image, and more awed by phenomenology vs. physiognomy. I have more
to say about what the mind knows than what the eye sees. I would rather
be inspired by dwelling in a place than be influenced by looking at an
object. Architecture for me is to create the void, not the solid. This
polarity distinguishes architecture as a discipline from architecture as
an industry. It also divides the history of architecture into two main
branches: the history of space and the history of form. One can as well
draw a line that separates the architects into two categories: the spatialist
who creates space with an impact that is lasting (think of ...), and the
formalist who builds object with a splash that is ephemeral (think of ...).
Of course, the division and the line do not deny the threshold and the
spectrum, where you can find all sort of quasi spatial / formal propositions:
X% spatial + Y% formal. With a higher X, you might be expecting an architecture with capital A that is poetic, while with a higher Y, at best,
you are dealing with an interesting building that is tectonic. This binary
analogy is quite helpful in differentiating between the two types:
the tactile one that starts with exploring a space and arrives at a form
— think of a cave — and the optical one that starts with inventing an image
or form and arrives at a space — think of a nest. Obviously, the latter
is the one that normally occurs when architects think of a design process,
building forms vs. forming spaces.

1

It is true that an image always sells better. Besides, we are curious creatures by nature, and, therefore, formal variation keeps us entertained and feeds our sense of excitement. Yet, everything we choose in life for its trendy look soon becomes outdated.This suggests a short lifespan, only a temporary high. Once we get bored we will either look for another ephemeral trend or wisely confront the closed loop and seek for a more enduring solution – often modest and humble – which can offer a refuge to our mind, a shelter to our body, and a sanctuary to our soul. Indeed, a profound space is capable to leave a long-lasting impact on us, while the interesting form leaves us with a sexy image that is good enough only to litter our memory. The former engraves a direct and deep experience that stays with us, a delightful recollection (always the same and always different); the latter makes a mental fatgue, a rubbish dump where it is very unlikely that any one among so many will succeed in standing out, a deceitful impression (always different and always the same).

It is the distinction between this polar opposites that makes me more interested in architecture as a discipline whose agenda is space-making vs. form-making, and its mandate is creating a spatial impact vs. a visual splash. The contrast also evokes in me the urge to constantly search, in order to find or invent methods which facilitate design strategies that allow me to create spaces that hold their autonomous internal orders rather than being by-products or leftovers of a formal gesture. In other words, in my projects I aim for the space, not the form, to be the protagonist.

I am very well aware of the fact that this might be an attempt beyond hope, to challenge what has become the normal, to confront the form and image making practice, to resist the temptation of market place, to set architecture free from being an industry, to release it from being a servant to commercial establishment, and to liberate it from the sick competition for visibility. All said, I would stay naive, and humbly invite you to join me bringing architecture back to the realm it belongs, where it deserves to be a passionate vocation to pursue, not a daily job to do, or as Le Corbusier always said, a habit of mind not a profession.
_ RZLBD (Reza Aliabadi)

Sep. + 2020 + Toronto

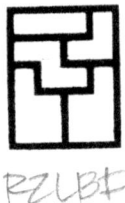

RZLBD

2

Letters To <u>Time</u>
140"
October 2020

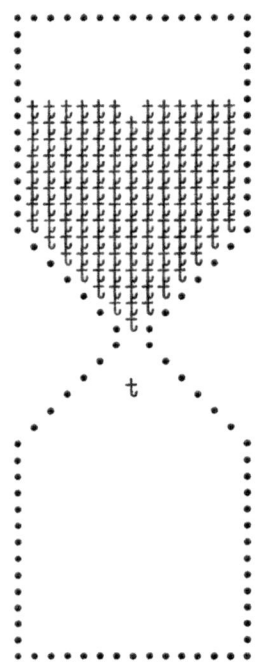

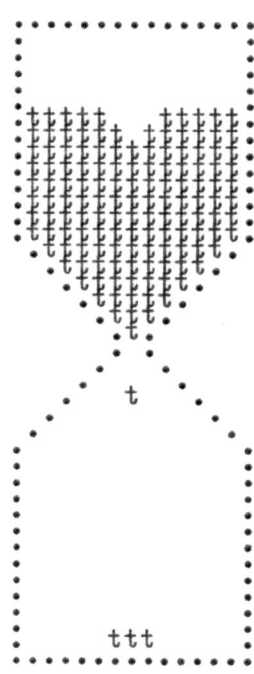

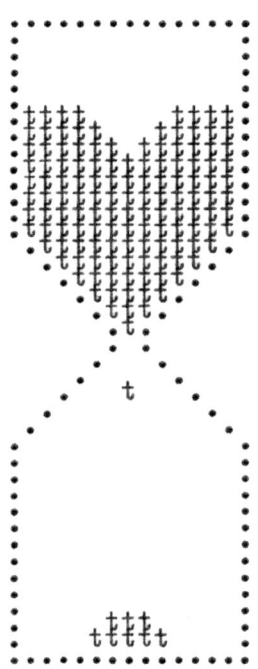

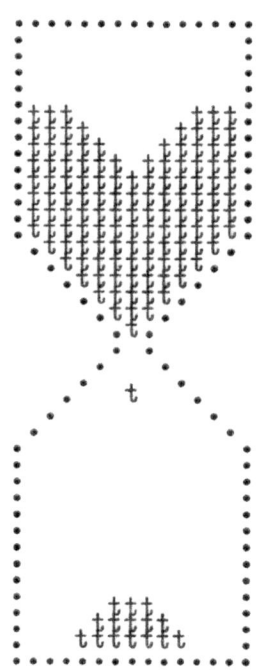

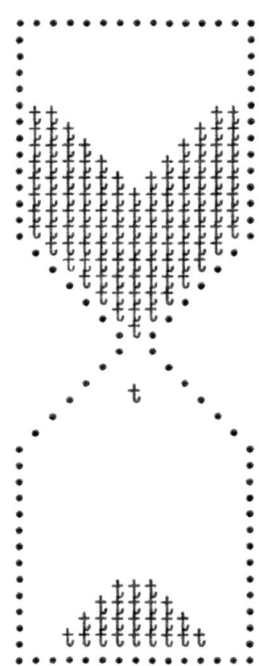

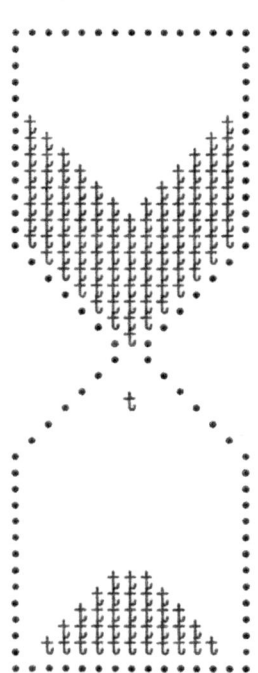

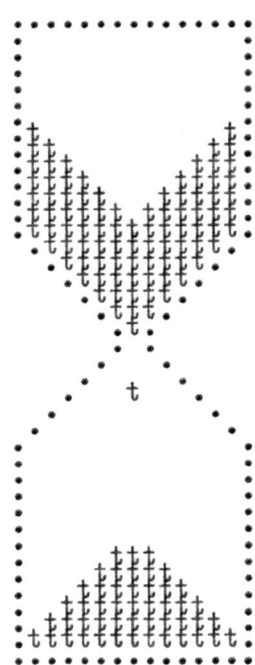

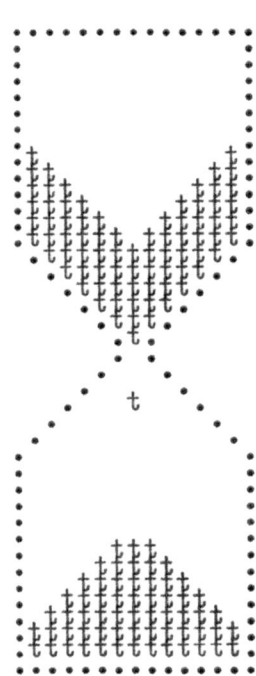

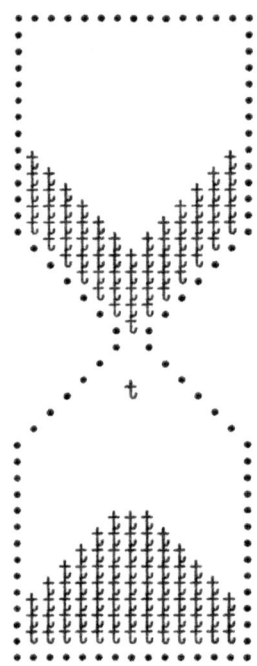

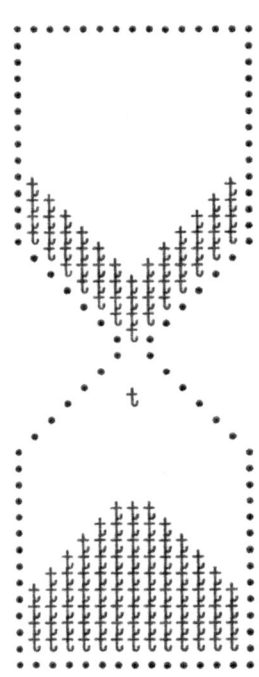

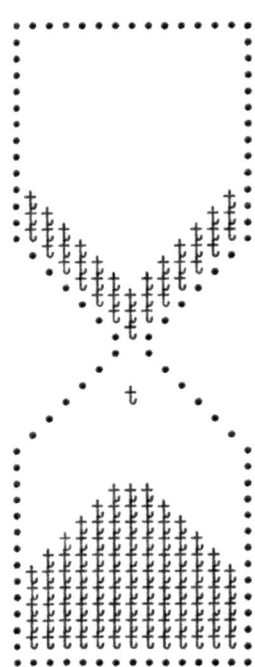

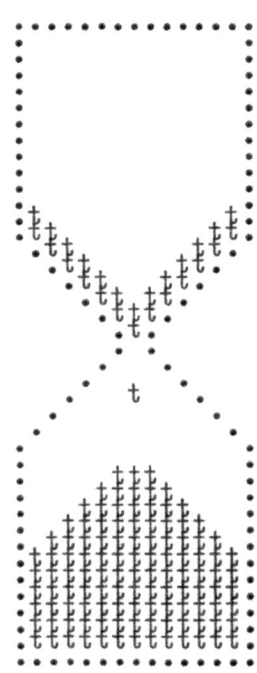

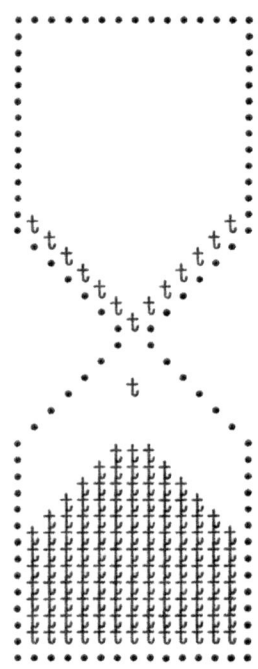

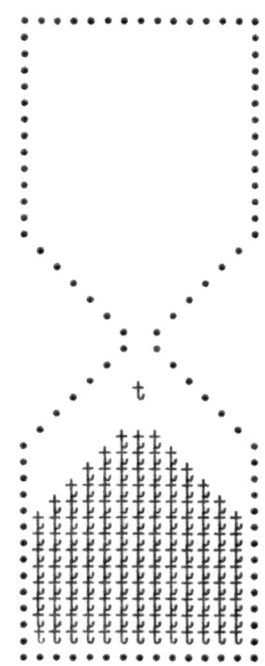

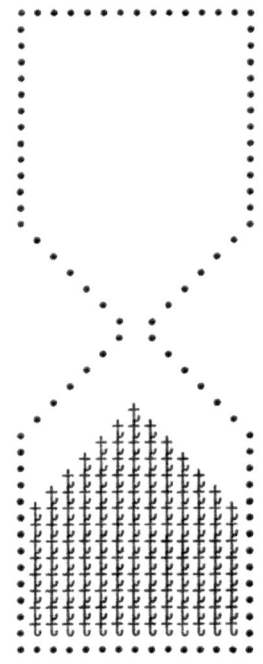

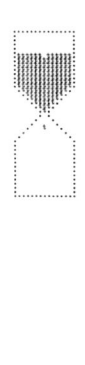 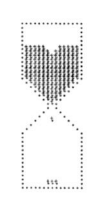 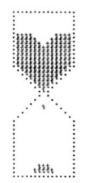 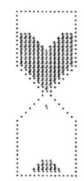 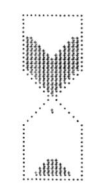

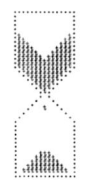 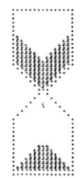 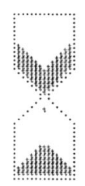 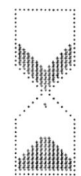 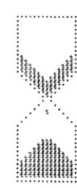

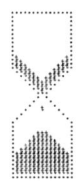 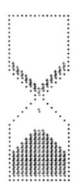 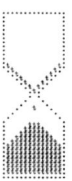 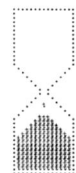 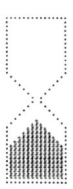

```
To    Yoko Ono
From  RZLBD
Date  22 Apr. 2021 (Earth Day)
No    5726 - 0030 B

EARTH PIECE
(dedicated to Yoko Ono)

Dear Yoko,

Write "I Love You Earth" 100 times.
Then cut them and send each one to a person you like.
Kindly ask them to repeat the same concept.
Until everyone in the world has one copy :)

I love you earth. I love you earth. I love you earth. I love you earth.
I love you earth. I love you earth. I love you earth. I love you earth.
I love you earth. I love you earth. I love you earth. I love you earth.
I love you earth. I love you earth. I love you earth. I love you earth.
I love you earth. I love you earth. I love you earth. I love you earth.
I love you earth. I love you earth. I love you earth. I love you earth.
I love you earth. I love you earth. I love you earth. I love you earth.
I love you earth. I love you earth. I love you earth. I love you earth.
I love you earth. I love you earth. I love you earth. I love you earth.
I love you earth. I love you earth. I love you earth. I love you earth.
I love you earth. I love you earth. I love you earth. I love you earth.
I love you earth. I love you earth. I love you earth. I love you earth.
I love you earth. I love you earth. I love you earth. I love you earth.
I love you earth. I love you earth. I love you earth. I love you earth.
I love you earth. I love you earth. I love you earth. I love you earth.
I love you earth. I love you earth. I love you earth. I love you earth.
I love you earth. I love you earth. I love you earth. I love you earth.
I love you earth. I love you earth. I love you earth. I love you earth.
I love you earth. I love you earth. I love you earth. I love you earth.
I love you earth. I love you earth. I love you earth. I love you earth.
I love you earth. I love you earth. I love you earth. I love you earth.
I love you earth. I love you earth. I love you earth. I love you earth.
I love you earth. I love you earth. I love you earth. I love you earth.
I love you earth. I love you earth. I love you earth. I love you earth.
I love you earth. I love you earth. I love you earth. I love you earth.

...

Hug & Kisses
RZLBD
```

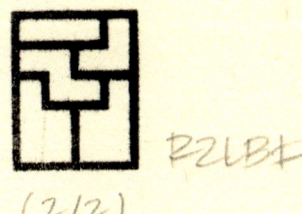

RZLBD

(2/2)

1000 Letters to <u>Pi</u>
07 May 2021

```
3.1415926535 8979323846 2643383279 5028841971 6939937510
  5820974944 5923078164 0628620899 8628034825 3421170679
  8214808651 3282306647 0938446095 5058223172 5359408128
  4811174502 8410270193 8521105559 6446229489 5493038196
  4428810975 6659334461 2847564823 3786783165 2712019091
  4564856692 3460348610 4543266482 1339360726 0249141273
  7245870066 0631558817 4881520920 9628292540 9171536436
  7892590360 0113305305 4882046652 1384146951 9415116094
  3305727036 5759591953 0921861173 8193261179 3105118548
  0744623799 6274956735 1885752724 8912279381 8301194912
  9833673362 4406566430 8602139494 6395224737 1907021798
  6094370277 0539217176 2931767523 8467481846 7669405132
  0005681271 4526356082 7785771342 7577896091 7363717872
  1468440901 2249534301 4654958537 1050792279 6892589235
  4201995611 2129021960 8640344181 5981362977 4771309960
  5187072113 4999999837 2978049951 0597317328 1609631859
  5024459455 3469083026 4252308225 3344685035 2619311881
  7101000313 7838752886 5875332083 8142061717 7669147303
  5982534904 2875546873 1159562863 8823537875 9375195778
  1857780532 1712268066 1300192787 6611195909 2164201989
```

•••

TBC

20 Letters to <u>Walter De Maria</u>
The Broken 100-m
or
20,000 (/)s
16 May 2021

/////////////////////////////////////////////
/////////////////////////////////////////////
/////////////////////////////////////////////
/////////////////////////////////////////////

/////////////////////////////////////////////
/////////////////////////////////////////////
/////////////////////////////////////////////
/////////////////////////////////////////////

/////////////////////////////////////////////
/////////////////////////////////////////////
/////////////////////////////////////////////
/////////////////////////////////////////////

/////////////////////////////////////////////
/////////////////////////////////////////////
/////////////////////////////////////////////
/////////////////////////////////////////////

/////////////////////////////////////////////
/////////////////////////////////////////////
/////////////////////////////////////////////
/////////////////////////////////////////////

01/20

/////////////////////////////////////////////
/////////////////////////////////////////////
/////////////////////////////////////////////
/////////////////////////////////////////////

/////////////////////////////////////////////
/////////////////////////////////////////////
/////////////////////////////////////////////
/////////////////////////////////////////////

/////////////////////////////////////////////
/////////////////////////////////////////////
/////////////////////////////////////////////
/////////////////////////////////////////////

/////////////////////////////////////////////
/////////////////////////////////////////////
/////////////////////////////////////////////
/////////////////////////////////////////////

/////////////////////////////////////////////
/////////////////////////////////////////////
/////////////////////////////////////////////
/////////////////////////////////////////////

02/20

////////////////////////////////////////////////
////////////////////////////////////////////////
////////////////////////////////////////////////
////////////////////////////////////////////////

////////////////////////////////////////////////
////////////////////////////////////////////////
////////////////////////////////////////////////
////////////////////////////////////////////////

////////////////////////////////////////////////
////////////////////////////////////////////////
////////////////////////////////////////////////
////////////////////////////////////////////////

////////////////////////////////////////////////
////////////////////////////////////////////////
////////////////////////////////////////////////
////////////////////////////////////////////////

////////////////////////////////////////////////
////////////////////////////////////////////////
////////////////////////////////////////////////
////////////////////////////////////////////////

03/20

/////////////////////////////////////////////
/////////////////////////////////////////////
/////////////////////////////////////////////
/////////////////////////////////////////////

/////////////////////////////////////////////
/////////////////////////////////////////////
/////////////////////////////////////////////
/////////////////////////////////////////////

/////////////////////////////////////////////
/////////////////////////////////////////////
/////////////////////////////////////////////
/////////////////////////////////////////////

/////////////////////////////////////////////
/////////////////////////////////////////////
/////////////////////////////////////////////
/////////////////////////////////////////////

/////////////////////////////////////////////
/////////////////////////////////////////////
/////////////////////////////////////////////
/////////////////////////////////////////////

04/20

////////////////////////////////////////////////
////////////////////////////////////////////////
////////////////////////////////////////////////
////////////////////////////////////////////////

////////////////////////////////////////////////
////////////////////////////////////////////////
////////////////////////////////////////////////
////////////////////////////////////////////////

////////////////////////////////////////////////
////////////////////////////////////////////////
////////////////////////////////////////////////
////////////////////////////////////////////////

////////////////////////////////////////////////
////////////////////////////////////////////////
////////////////////////////////////////////////
////////////////////////////////////////////////

////////////////////////////////////////////////
////////////////////////////////////////////////
////////////////////////////////////////////////
////////////////////////////////////////////////

05/20

///////////////////////////////////////////////
///////////////////////////////////////////////
///////////////////////////////////////////////
///////////////////////////////////////////////

///////////////////////////////////////////////
///////////////////////////////////////////////
///////////////////////////////////////////////
///////////////////////////////////////////////

///////////////////////////////////////////////
///////////////////////////////////////////////
///////////////////////////////////////////////
///////////////////////////////////////////////

///////////////////////////////////////////////
///////////////////////////////////////////////
///////////////////////////////////////////////
///////////////////////////////////////////////

///////////////////////////////////////////////
///////////////////////////////////////////////
///////////////////////////////////////////////
///////////////////////////////////////////////

06/20

////////////////////////////////////////////////////
////////////////////////////////////////////////////
////////////////////////////////////////////////////
//////////////////////////////////////////////////

////////////////////////////////////////////////////
////////////////////////////////////////////////////
////////////////////////////////////////////////////
////////////////////////////////////////////////////

////////////////////////////////////////////////////
////////////////////////////////////////////////////
////////////////////////////////////////////////////
////////////////////////////////////////////////////

////////////////////////////////////////////////////
////////////////////////////////////////////////////
////////////////////////////////////////////////////
////////////////////////////////////////////////////

////////////////////////////////////////////////////
////////////////////////////////////////////////////
////////////////////////////////////////////////////
////////////////////////////////////////////////////

07/20

////////////////////////////////////////////////
////////////////////////////////////////////////
////////////////////////////////////////////////
////////////////////////////////////////////////

////////////////////////////////////////////////
////////////////////////////////////////////////
////////////////////////////////////////////////
////////////////////////////////////////////////

////////////////////////////////////////////////
////////////////////////////////////////////////
////////////////////////////////////////////////
////////////////////////////////////////////////

////////////////////////////////////////////////
////////////////////////////////////////////////
////////////////////////////////////////////////
////////////////////////////////////////////////

////////////////////////////////////////////////
////////////////////////////////////////////////
////////////////////////////////////////////////
////////////////////////////////////////////////

08/20

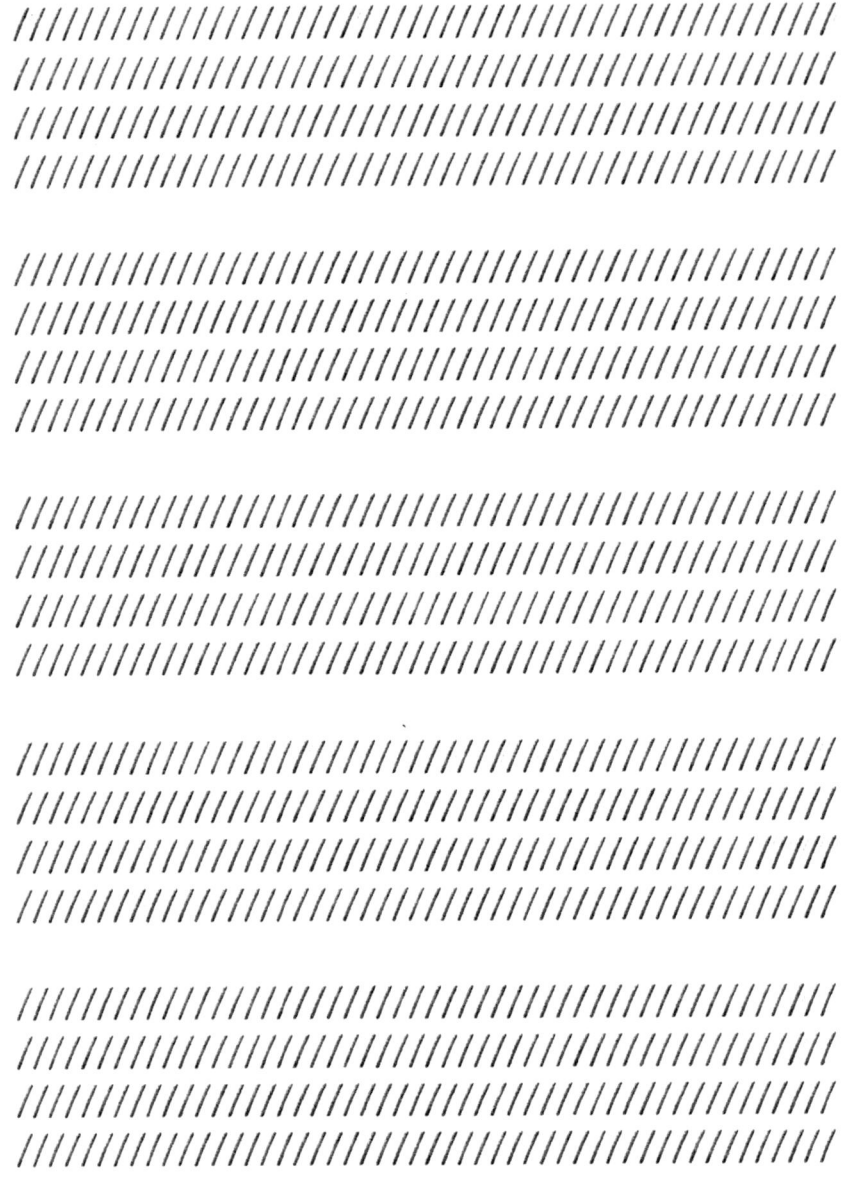

09/20

/////////////////////////////////////////////
/////////////////////////////////////////////
/////////////////////////////////////////////
/////////////////////////////////////////////

/////////////////////////////////////////////
/////////////////////////////////////////////
/////////////////////////////////////////////
/////////////////////////////////////////////

/////////////////////////////////////////////
/////////////////////////////////////////////
/////////////////////////////////////////////
/////////////////////////////////////////////

/////////////////////////////////////////////
/////////////////////////////////////////////
/////////////////////////////////////////////
/////////////////////////////////////////////

/////////////////////////////////////////////
/////////////////////////////////////////////
////////////////////////////////////////////
/////////////////////////////////////////////

10/20

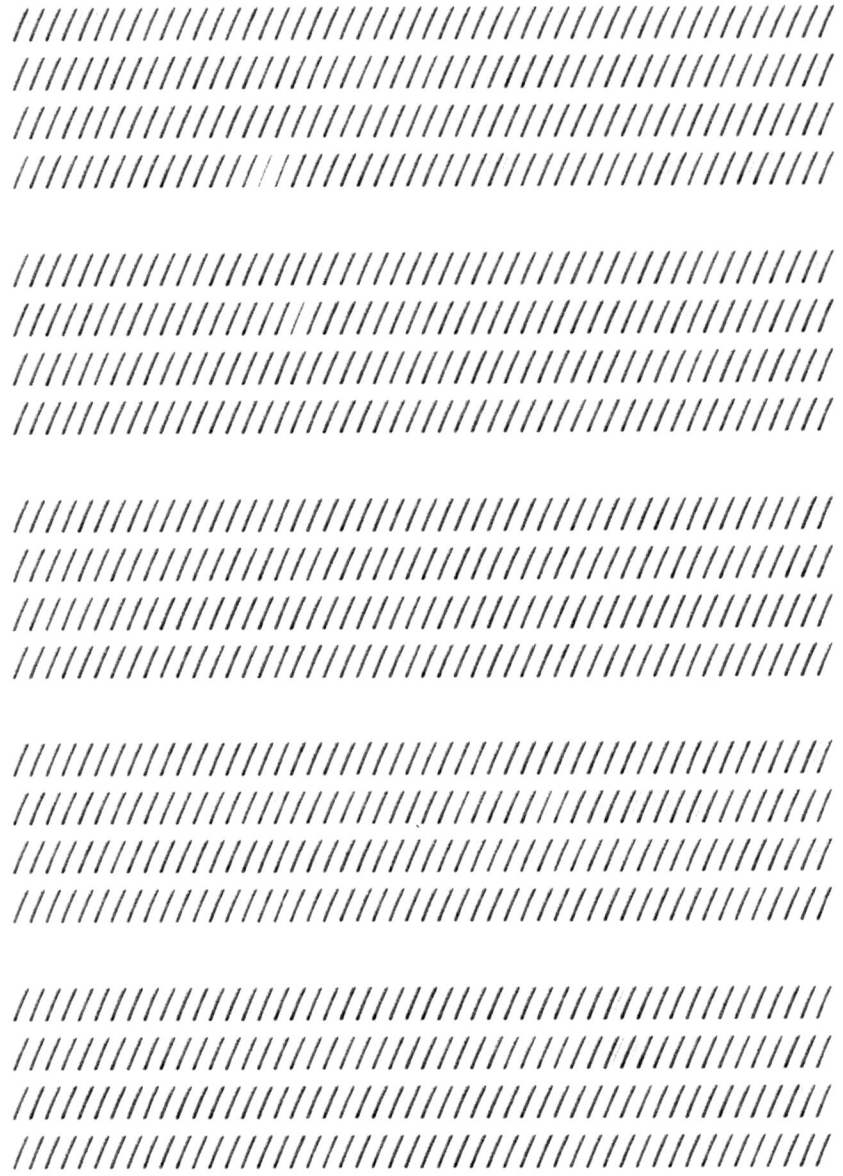

11/20

////////////////////////////////////////////////
////////////////////////////////////////////////
////////////////////////////////////////////////
////////////////////////////////////////////////

////////////////////////////////////////////////
////////////////////////////////////////////////
////////////////////////////////////////////////
////////////////////////////////////////////////

////////////////////////////////////////////////
////////////////////////////////////////////////
////////////////////////////////////////////////
////////////////////////////////////////////////

////////////////////////////////////////////////
////////////////////////////////////////////////
////////////////////////////////////////////////
////////////////////////////////////////////////

////////////////////////////////////////////////
////////////////////////////////////////////////
////////////////////////////////////////////////
////////////////////////////////////////////////

12/20

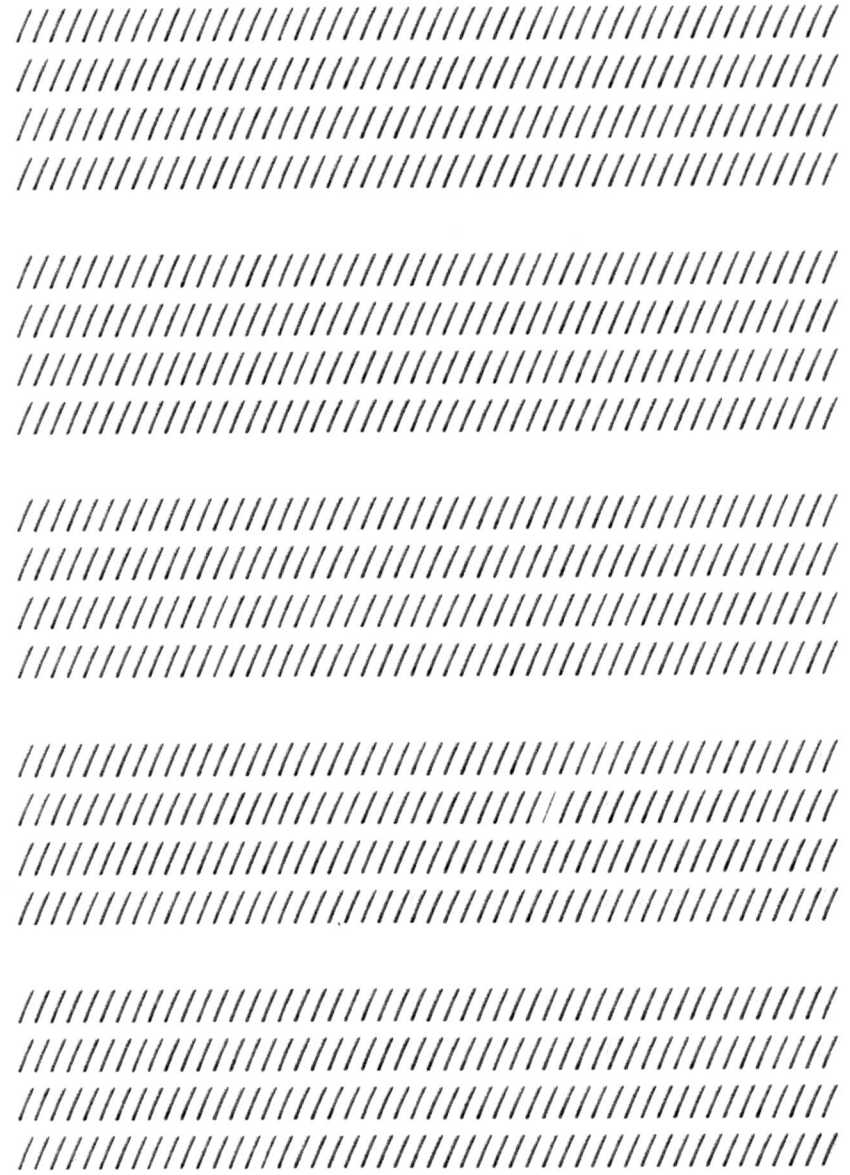

13/20

/////////////////////////////////////////////
/////////////////////////////////////////////
/////////////////////////////////////////////
/////////////////////////////////////////////

/////////////////////////////////////////////
/////////////////////////////////////////////
/////////////////////////////////////////////
/////////////////////////////////////////////

/////////////////////////////////////////////
/////////////////////////////////////////////
/////////////////////////////////////////////
/////////////////////////////////////////////

/////////////////////////////////////////////
/////////////////////////////////////////////
/////////////////////////////////////////////
/////////////////////////////////////////////

/////////////////////////////////////////////
/////////////////////////////////////////////
/////////////////////////////////////////////
/////////////////////////////////////////////

14/20

/////////////////////////////////////////////////
/////////////////////////////////////////////////
/////////////////////////////////////////////////
/////////////////////////////////////////////////

/////////////////////////////////////////////////
/////////////////////////////////////////////////
/////////////////////////////////////////////////
/////////////////////////////////////////////////

/////////////////////////////////////////////////
/////////////////////////////////////////////////
/////////////////////////////////////////////////
/////////////////////////////////////////////////

/////////////////////////////////////////////////
/////////////////////////////////////////////////
/////////////////////////////////////////////////
/////////////////////////////////////////////////

/////////////////////////////////////////////////
/////////////////////////////////////////////////
/////////////////////////////////////////////////
/////////////////////////////////////////////////

15/20

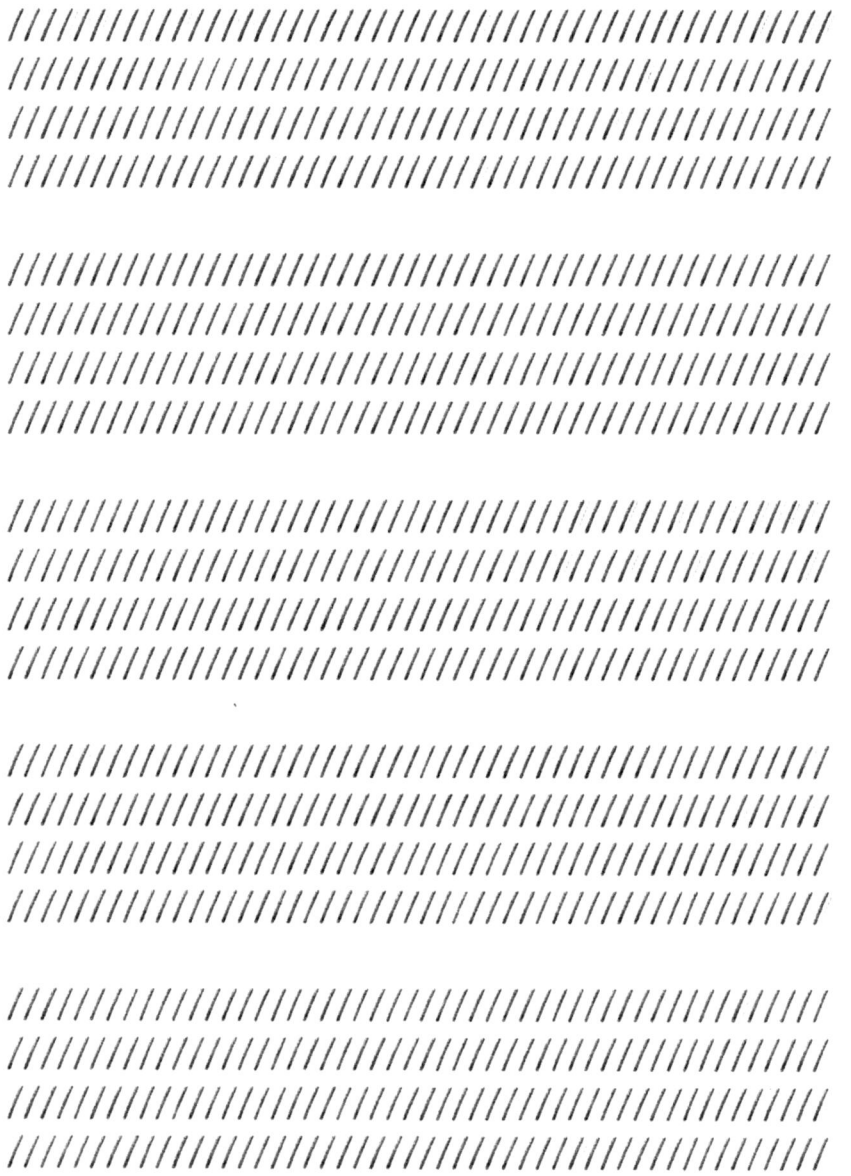

16/20

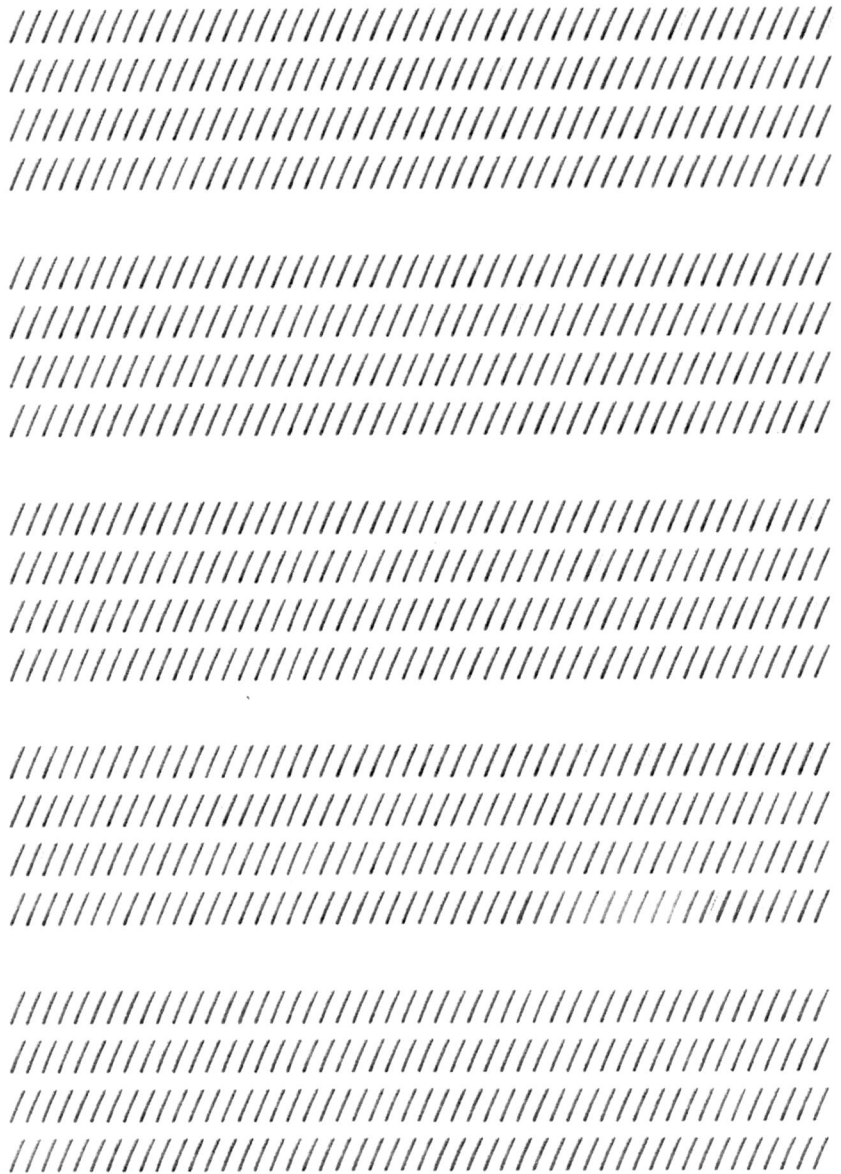

//////////////////////////////////////////////////
//////////////////////////////////////////////////
//////////////////////////////////////////////////
//////////////////////////////////////////////////

//////////////////////////////////////////////////
//////////////////////////////////////////////////
//////////////////////////////////////////////////
//////////////////////////////////////////////////

//////////////////////////////////////////////////
//////////////////////////////////////////////////
//////////////////////////////////////////////////
//////////////////////////////////////////////////

//////////////////////////////////////////////////
//////////////////////////////////////////////////
//////////////////////////////////////////////////
//////////////////////////////////////////////////

//////////////////////////////////////////////////
//////////////////////////////////////////////////
//////////////////////////////////////////////////
//////////////////////////////////////////////////

18/20

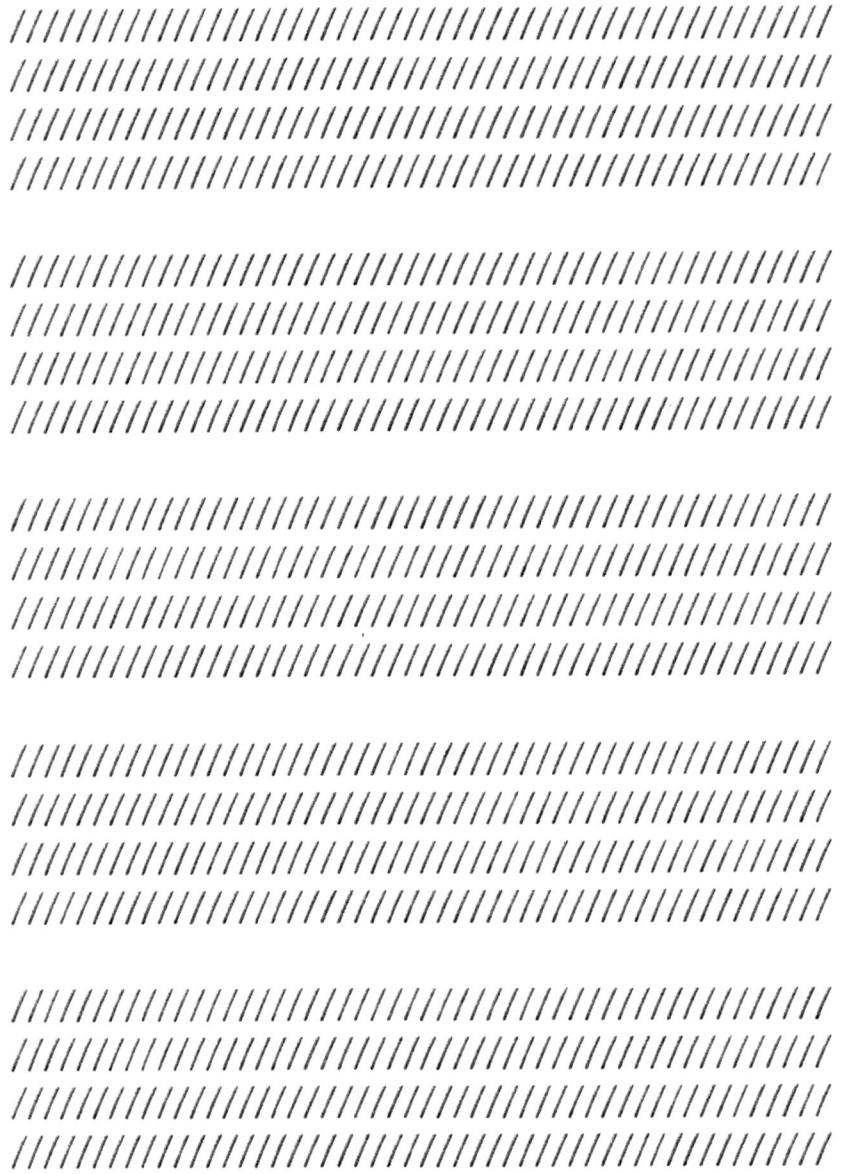

19/20

////////////////////////////////////////////
////////////////////////////////////////////
///////////////////////////////////////////////
////////////////////////////////////////////

////////////////////////////////////////////
////////////////////////////////////////////
////////////////////////////////////////////
////////////////////////////////////////////

////////////////////////////////////////////
////////////////////////////////////////////
////////////////////////////////////////////
////////////////////////////////////////////

////////////////////////////////////////////
////////////////////////////////////////////
////////////////////////////////////////////
////////////////////////////////////////////

////////////////////////////////////////////
////////////////////////////////////////////
////////////////////////////////////////////
////////////////////////////////////////////

20/20

Letter to Siah Armajani
19 May 2021

Siah (Siavash) Armajani: ~~(Persian, 10 July 1939 – 27 August 2020)~~
~~was an Iranian-American sculptor and architect known for his~~
~~public art.~~

~~Family and education~~
~~Siavash Armajani was born into a wealthy, educated family of textile~~
~~merchants in 1939 in Tehran, Iran. He attended a Presbyterian~~
~~missionary school. He thought that his grandmother was the influence~~
~~that started his political activism. He began his art career making~~
~~small collages in the late 1950s, visually mirroring Persian miniatures~~
~~and political posters, to spread his vision of democracy and secularism~~
~~and to publicize his party, the National Front.~~

~~After the monarch Shah Mohammad Reza Pahlavi came to power, in order to~~
~~protect him, his family ordered him overseas in 1960. Armajani then~~
~~immigrated to the United States, where his uncle, Yahya Armajani, was~~
~~chair of the history department at Macalester College. There he studied~~
~~art and philosophy, making Saint Paul, Minnesota, his permanent home.~~
~~He met his wife at Macalester and he and Barbara Bauer married in 1966.~~
~~He became an American citizen in 1967.~~

~~Early career~~
~~The Walker Art Center was the first to acquire Armajani's work, after~~
~~he entered two works into their biennial in 1968. They purchased Prayer,~~
~~an intricately lettered 70-inch (180 cm) canvas covered in Farsi poetry.~~

~~Always interested in computing and engineering, during the late 1960s~~
~~he took classes at Control Data Institute in Minneapolis where he~~
~~learned Fortran. Armajani taught at the Minneapolis College of Art &~~
~~Design from 1968 until 1974, where he met Barry Le Va, who introduced~~
~~him to conceptual art then practiced in New York City. He participated~~
~~in Art by Telegraph at the Museum of Contemporary Art, Chicago in 1969.~~
~~In 1970, Armajani contributed two works to the Museum of Modern Art~~
~~exhibition Information: first, A Number Between Zero and One, a 9-foot~~
~~(2.7 m) high column filled with computer printout of individual decimal~~
~~numbers, and second, North Dakota Tower, a proposed pipe 18 miles~~
~~(29 km) high and 2 miles (3.2 km) wide calculated to cast a narrow~~
~~shadow across the entire length of North Dakota from east to west.~~

1/3

Bridges

## Later career

In his later years, Armajani returned to his politically active roots. His 2005 work, Fallujah, is a modern take on Picasso's Guernica but was censored in the U.S. due to its critical view of the war in Iraq. It was recently on view at the Walker Art Center in Minneapolis, Minnesota. Seven Rooms of Hospitality is based on a conversation between Jacques Derrida and Anne Dufourmantelle. Room for Deportees (2017) speaks out to the hard-line, anti-immigrant policies the took over in the U.S. and Europe.

An exhibition at Nuclear...on Gallery in 2011 presented a dozen of Armajani's early pieces made between 1957 and 1962, created in the years leading up to his arrival in America. Many employ ink or water color on cloth or paper, and incorporate text. In his Shirt (1958), 5... feet (1.5 m) fabric, Armajani uses pencil and ink to completely cover his father's shirt in Persian script.

The Minneapolis Institute of Art holds several works, Skyway No 3 (1980), Mississippi Delta (2005–2006), a colored pencil on Mylar triptych picturing the aftermath of Hurricane Katrina, and An Exile Dreaming of Saint Adorno (2009), a cage-like inhabited tiny house... a...garage named for Theodor W. Adorno.

Armajani was the subject of more than 50 solo exhibitions, and his works featured in dozens of major exhibitions in the U.S. and Europe. Siah Armajani: Follow This Line, the first comprehensive U.S. retrospective dedicated to the artist, was on view at the Walker Art Center September 9 through December 30, 2018, and at the Met Breuer February 20 through June 2, 2019.

## Death

Armajani died of heart failure in Minneapolis on August 27, 2020, at age 81.

## Awards and honors

In 2010, he won a Knight Fellow award granted by United States Artists. In 2011, he was awarded Chevalier of the Order des Arts et des Lettres by the French government and received a distinguished artist award from the McKnight Foundation.

3/3

Letter to <u>Richard Serra</u>
Verb List, 1967 – 68
23 May 2021

to roll to curve
to crease to lift
to fold to inlay
to store to impress
to bend to fire
to shorten to flood
to twist to smear
to dapple to rotate
to crumple to swirl
to shave to support
to tear to hook
to chip to suspend
to split to spread
to cut to hang
to sever to collect
to drop of tension
to remove of gravity
to simplify of entropy
to differ of nature
to disarrange of grouping
to open of layering
to mix of felting
to splash to grasp
to knot to tighten
to spill to bundle
to droop to heap
to flow to gather

1/2

140

to scatter          to modulate
to arrange          to distill
to repair           of waves
to discard          of electromagnetic
to pair             of inertia
to distribute       of ionization
to surfeit          of polarization
to complement       of refraction
to enclose          of simultaneity
to surround         of tides
to encircle         of reflection
to hide             of equilibrium
to cover            of symmetry
to wrap             of friction
to dig              to stretch
to tie              to bounce
to bind             to erase
to weave            to spray
to join             to systematize
to match            to refer
to laminate         to force
to bond             of mapping
to hinge            of location
to mark             of context
to expand           of time
to dilute           of carbonization
to light            to continue

2/2

```
To    On Kawara
From  RZLBD
Date  31 May, 2021
No    5726 - 0030 A
```

MAY: A MONTH IT WAS

I am still alive.

| My Day<br>May 2021 | My Luck<br>Rolling Dice | My finance<br>Gas Price (CAD) |
|---|---|---|
| 01 | 6 & 5 | 131.90 |
| 02 | 4 & 3 | 129.90 |
| 03 | 6 & 1 | 129.90 |
| 04 | 6 & 2 | 129.90 |
| 05 | 4 & 2 | 130.90 |
| 06 | 4 & 1 | 133.90 (H) |
| 07 | 6 & 5 | 132.90 |
| 08 | 6 & 5 | 130.90 |
| 09 | 6 & 5 | 130.90 |
| 10 | 3 & 1 | 130.90 |
| 11 | 3 & 3 | 130.90 |
| 12 | 5 & 1 | 130.90 |
| 13 | 4 & 3 | 130.90 |
| 14 | 6 & 4 | 131.90 |
| 15 | 6 & 2 | 129.90 |
| 16 | 3 & 1 | 130.90 |
| 17 | 6 & 3 | 130.90 |
| 18 | 4 & 1 | 130.90 |
| 19 | 2 & 2 | 131.90 |
| 20 | 1 & 1 | 131.90 |
| 21 | 4 & 2 | 129.90 |
| 22 | 3 & 1 | 127.90 (L) |
| 23 | 5 & 1 | 127.90 (L) |
| 24 | 6 & 6 | 128.90 |
| 25 | 6 & 2 | 128.90 |
| 26 | 6 & 4 | 128.90 |
| 27 | 6 & 6 | 129.90 |
| 28 | 3 & 2 | 131.90 |
| 29 | 5 & 2 | 131.90 |
| 30 | 6 & 3 | 130.90 |
| 31 | 5 & 1 | 130.90 |

I am going to sleep now.

Humbly Yours,
RZLBD

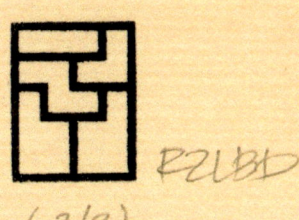

(2/2)

Letters To My Luck
365 Days
Sep. 2020 To Sep. 2021

SEP 2020

```
01  -
02  -
03  -
04  -
05  -
06  -
07  -
08  -
09  -
10  -
11  -
12  -
13  -
14  -
15  -
16  -
17  -
18  -
19  -
20  -
21  -
22  -
23  -
24  -
25  -
26  -
27  -
28  -
29  5 & 3
30  3 & 1
```

OCT 2020

```
01   6 & 5
02   4 & 1
03   6 & 3
04   5 & 1
05   3 & 2
06   5 & 2
07   6 & 2
08   6 & 2
09   6 & 5
10   6 & 5
11   6 & 1
12   2 & 1
13   5 & 3
14   2 & 1
15   3 & 2
16   2 & 2
17   5 & 5
18   5 & 2
19   3 & 1
20   6 & 4
21   4 & 1
22   6 & 6
23   6 & 6
24   4 & 2
25   2 & 2
26   6 & 1
27   6 & 4
28   3 & 2
29   4 & 1
30   6 & 6
31   5 & 1
```

NOV 2020

```
01   5 & 1
02   5 & 2
03   5 & 3
04   4 & 4
05   6 & 6
06   4 & 1
07   4 & 3
08   2 & 1
09   4 & 2
10   6 & 4
11   6 & 5
12   6 & 2
13   5 & 1
14   1 & 1
15   3 & 1
16   4 & 2
17   5 & 1
18   3 & 1
19   6 & 4
20   5 & 3
21   6 & 3
22   6 & 4
23   6 & 4
24   4 & 1
25   5 & 2
26   6 & 6
27   5 & 4
28   3 & 1
29   6 & 2
30   6 & 3
```

DEC 2020

```
01   6 & 2
02   5 & 3
03   6 & 3
04   4 & 3
05   6 & 1
06   4 & 4
07   5 & 3
08   3 & 2
09   6 & 4
10   5 & 2
11   6 & 3
12   5 & 1
13   4 & 3
14   5 & 3
15   5 & 3
16   6 & 2
17   3 & 2
18   5 & 3
19   2 & 1
20   5 & 4
21   6 & 6
22   5 & 5
23   5 & 2
24   6 & 1
25   5 & 3
26   5 & 1
27   3 & 3
28   6 & 6
29   4 & 3
30   6 & 1
31   1 & 1
```

JAN 2021

| | | | |
|---|---|---|---|
| 01 | 3 | & | 3 |
| 02 | 5 | & | 1 |
| 03 | 5 | & | 4 |
| 04 | 2 | & | 1 |
| 05 | 3 | & | 1 |
| 06 | 6 | & | 1 |
| 07 | 4 | & | 3 |
| 08 | 3 | & | 2 |
| 09 | 6 | & | 1 |
| 10 | 4 | & | 1 |
| 11 | 6 | & | 5 |
| 12 | 5 | & | 1 |
| 13 | 4 | & | 3 |
| 14 | 2 | & | 2 |
| 15 | 4 | & | 3 |
| 16 | 4 | & | 2 |
| 17 | 6 | & | 1 |
| 18 | 6 | & | 3 |
| 19 | 6 | & | 5 |
| 20 | 6 | & | 1 |
| 21 | 6 | & | 2 |
| 22 | 3 | & | 1 |
| 23 | 3 | & | 1 |
| 24 | 4 | & | 2 |
| 25 | 4 | & | 3 |
| 26 | 5 | & | 1 |
| 27 | 6 | & | 4 |
| 28 | 3 | & | 3 |
| 29 | 4 | & | 2 |
| 30 | 5 | & | 2 |
| 31 | 4 | & | 3 |

150

FEB 2021

```
01   6 & 1
02   2 & 2
03   6 & 5
04   3 & 3
05   6 & 3
06   5 & 4
07   6 & 4
08   4 & 3
09   6 & 4
10   6 & 5
11   4 & 3
12   5 & 1
13   2 & 2
14   6 & 3
15   5 & 1
16   6 & 6
17   4 & 3
18   4 & 1
19   4 & 3
20   4 & 4
21   6 & 4
22   6 & 4
23   6 & 6
24   5 & 5
25   5 & 4
26   4 & 1
27   5 & 4
28   3 & 2
```

MAR 2021

| | | | |
|---|---|---|---|
| 01 | 4 | & | 4 |
| 02 | 5 | & | 3 |
| 03 | 3 | & | 1 |
| 04 | 2 | & | 2 |
| 05 | 5 | & | 3 |
| 06 | 6 | & | 4 |
| 07 | 3 | & | 3 |
| 08 | 5 | & | 1 |
| 09 | 4 | & | 2 |
| 10 | 4 | & | 2 |
| 11 | 2 | & | 1 |
| 12 | 3 | & | 3 |
| 13 | 6 | & | 1 |
| 14 | 3 | & | 3 |
| 15 | 4 | & | 3 |
| 16 | 4 | & | 3 |
| 17 | 6 | & | 4 |
| 18 | 6 | & | 1 |
| 19 | 6 | & | 5 |
| 20 | 6 | & | 2 |
| 21 | 4 | & | 2 |
| 22 | 3 | & | 3 |
| 23 | 5 | & | 4 |
| 24 | 6 | & | 4 |
| 25 | 6 | & | 4 |
| 26 | 5 | & | 3 |
| 27 | 5 | & | 4 |
| 28 | 3 | & | 2 |
| 29 | 4 | & | 2 |
| 30 | 5 | & | 5 |
| 31 | 6 | & | 3 |

APR 2021

| | | |
|---|---|---|
| 01 | 6 & | 4 |
| 02 | 3 & | 2 |
| 03 | 4 & | 2 |
| 04 | 6 & | 5 |
| 05 | 6 & | 1 |
| 06 | 4 & | 1 |
| 07 | 4 & | 4 |
| 08 | 5 & | 4 |
| 09 | 6 & | 4 |
| 10 | 5 & | 4 |
| 11 | 5 & | 4 |
| 12 | 6 & | 5 |
| 13 | 4 & | 1 |
| 14 | 3 & | 2 |
| 15 | 5 & | 1 |
| 16 | 6 & | 2 |
| 17 | 1 & | 1 |
| 18 | 6 & | 1 |
| 19 | 6 & | 5 |
| 20 | 5 & | 3 |
| 21 | 5 & | 2 |
| 22 | 5 & | 1 |
| 23 | 5 & | 2 |
| 24 | 6 & | 2 |
| 25 | 2 & | 1 |
| 26 | 5 & | 1 |
| 27 | 3 & | 2 |
| 28 | 6 & | 3 |
| 29 | 6 & | 3 |
| 30 | 6 & | 2 |

MAY 2021

```
01   6 & 5
02   4 & 3
03   6 & 1
04   6 & 2
05   4 & 2
06   4 & 1
07   6 & 5
08   6 & 5
09   6 & 5
10   3 & 1
11   3 & 3
12   5 & 1
13   4 & 3
14   6 & 4
15   6 & 2
16   3 & 1
17   6 & 3
18   4 & 1
19   2 & 2
20   1 & 1
21   4 & 2
22   3 & 1
23   5 & 1
24   6 & 6
25   6 & 2
26   6 & 4
27   6 & 6
28   3 & 2
29   5 & 2
30   6 & 3
31   5 & 1
```

154

JUN 2021

01   3 & 3
02   5 & 1
03   6 & 1
04   4 & 1
05   6 & 6
06   5 & 4
07   4 & 1
08   5 & 2
09   6 & 5
10   6 & 5
11   5 & 3
12   4 & 2
13   6 & 2
14   3 & 1
15   4 & 3
16   5 & 3
17   6 & 1
18   3 & 3
19   4 & 1
20   6 & 11
21   6 & 5
22   2 & 1
23   5 & 4
24   3 & 2
25   6 & 6
26   4 & 3
27   5 & 3
28   3 & 1
29   4 & 2
30   6 & 3

JUL 2021

```
01   6 & 1
02   2 & 2
03   2 & 2
04   6 & 4
05   4 & 4
06   4 & 2
07   5 & 3
08   6 & 2
09   6 & 2
10   6 & 4
11   3 & 1
12   6 & 1
13   6 & 1
14   6 & 2
15   5 & 2
16   2 & 1
17   6 & 1
18   6 & 3
19   6 & 6
20   1 & 1
21   6 & 6
22   4 & 3
23   5 & 3
24   3 & 1
25   3 & 1
26   6 & 2
27   6 & 3
28   5 & 2
29   6 & 2
30   5 & 2
31   6 & 2
```

AUG 2021

```
01   4 & 3
02   2 & 1
03   6 & 2
04   3 & 2
05   4 & 4
06   6 & 1
07   6 & 6
08   6 & 6
09   5 & 2
10   5 & 6
11   3 & 1
12   2 & 2
13   6 & 6
14   4 & 1
15   5 & 3
16   6 & 2
17   5 & 4
18   6 & 2
19   4 & 1
20   6 & 1
21   6 & 2
22   5 & 2
23   6 & 2
24   4 & 2
25   6 & 1
26   5 & 4
27   6 & 5
28   4 & 1
29   4 & 3
30   6 & 1
31   6 & 3
```

SEP 2021

| | | | |
|---|---|---|---|
| 01 | 3 | & | 2 |
| 02 | 6 | & | 1 |
| 03 | 1 | & | 1 |
| 04 | 6 | & | 5 |
| 05 | 6 | & | 2 |
| 06 | 2 | & | 2 |
| 07 | 6 | & | 2 |
| 08 | 6 | & | 2 |
| 09 | 5 | & | 4 |
| 10 | 3 | & | 1 |
| 11 | 3 | & | 2 |
| 12 | 4 | & | 4 |
| 13 | 6 | & | 1 |
| 14 | 6 | & | 6 |
| 15 | 6 | & | 4 |
| 16 | 6 | & | 2 |
| 17 | 5 | & | 4 |
| 18 | 3 | & | 2 |
| 19 | 4 | & | 4 |
| 20 | 6 | & | 3 |
| 21 | 6 | & | 1 |
| 22 | 3 | & | 1 |
| 23 | 6 | & | 3 |
| 24 | 6 | & | 2 |
| 25 | 6 | & | 1 |
| 26 | 6 | & | 1 |
| 27 | 2 | & | 1 |
| 28 | 5 | & | 4 |
| 29 | – | | |
| 30 | – | | |

158

| Day | SEP 2020 | OCT 2020 | NOV 2020 | DEC 2020 | JAN 2021 | FEB 2021 | MAR 2021 | APR 2021 | MAY 2021 | JUN 2021 | JUL 2021 | AUG 2021 | SEP 2021 |
|---|---|---|---|---|---|---|---|---|---|---|---|---|---|
| 01 | – | 6 & 5 | 5 & 1 | 6 & 2 | 3 & 3 | 6 & 1 | 4 & 4 | 6 & 4 | 6 & 5 | 3 & 3 | 6 & 1 | 4 & 3 | 3 & 2 |
| 02 | – | 5 & 2 | 5 & 2 | 5 & 3 | 5 & 1 | 2 & 2 | 5 & 3 | 3 & 2 | 4 & 3 | 5 & 1 | 2 & 2 | 2 & 1 | 6 & 1 |
| 03 | – | 6 & 3 | 5 & 3 | 6 & 3 | 5 & 4 | 6 & 5 | 3 & 1 | 4 & 2 | 6 & 1 | 6 & 1 | 2 & 1 | 6 & 2 | 1 & 1 |
| 04 | – | 5 & 1 | 4 & 4 | 4 & 3 | 2 & 1 | 3 & 3 | 2 & 2 | 6 & 5 | 6 & 2 | 4 & 1 | 6 & 4 | 3 & 2 | 6 & 3 |
| 05 | – | 3 & 2 | 6 & 6 | 6 & 1 | 3 & 1 | 6 & 3 | 5 & 3 | 4 & 2 | 4 & 2 | 6 & 6 | 4 & 4 | 4 & 4 | 6 & 2 |
| 06 | – | 5 & 2 | 4 & 1 | 4 & 4 | 6 & 1 | 5 & 4 | 6 & 4 | 4 & 1 | 4 & 1 | 5 & 4 | 4 & 2 | 6 & 1 | 2 & 2 |
| 07 | – | 6 & 2 | 4 & 3 | 5 & 3 | 4 & 3 | 6 & 4 | 3 & 3 | 4 & 4 | 6 & 5 | 4 & 1 | 5 & 3 | 6 & 6 | 6 & 2 |
| 08 | – | 6 & 2 | 2 & 1 | 3 & 2 | 3 & 2 | 4 & 3 | 3 & 3 | 5 & 4 | 6 & 5 | 5 & 2 | 5 & 2 | 6 & 6 | 6 & 2 |
| 09 | – | 6 & 5 | 4 & 2 | 6 & 4 | 6 & 1 | 6 & 4 | 5 & 1 | 6 & 4 | 6 & 5 | 6 & 5 | 6 & 2 | 5 & 2 | 5 & 4 |
| 10 | – | 6 & 5 | 6 & 4 | 5 & 2 | 4 & 1 | 6 & 5 | 4 & 2 | 5 & 4 | 3 & 1 | 6 & 4 | 6 & 4 | 5 & 6 | 3 & 1 |
| 11 | – | 6 & 1 | 6 & 5 | 6 & 3 | 6 & 5 | 4 & 3 | 2 & 1 | 2 & 1 | 5 & 4 | 3 & 1 | 3 & 1 | 3 & 1 | 3 & 2 |
| 12 | – | 2 & 1 | 6 & 2 | 5 & 1 | 5 & 1 | 5 & 1 | 3 & 3 | 6 & 5 | 5 & 1 | 4 & 2 | 3 & 1 | 2 & 2 | 2 & 2 |
| 13 | – | 5 & 3 | 5 & 1 | 4 & 3 | 4 & 3 | 2 & 2 | 6 & 1 | 4 & 1 | 4 & 1 | 6 & 2 | 6 & 2 | 6 & 6 | 6 & 1 |
| 14 | – | 2 & 1 | 1 & 1 | 5 & 3 | 2 & 2 | 6 & 3 | 3 & 3 | 3 & 2 | 6 & 4 | 3 & 1 | 6 & 2 | 4 & 1 | 6 & 6 |
| 15 | – | 3 & 2 | 3 & 1 | 5 & 3 | 4 & 3 | 5 & 1 | 4 & 3 | 5 & 1 | 5 & 1 | 5 & 3 | 6 & 2 | 5 & 3 | 5 & 4 |
| 16 | – | 2 & 2 | 4 & 2 | 6 & 2 | 4 & 2 | 6 & 6 | 4 & 3 | 6 & 2 | 6 & 2 | 2 & 1 | 2 & 1 | 6 & 2 | 6 & 2 |
| 17 | – | 5 & 5 | 5 & 1 | 3 & 2 | 6 & 1 | 4 & 3 | 6 & 4 | 1 & 1 | 6 & 3 | 6 & 1 | 6 & 1 | 5 & 4 | 5 & 4 |
| 18 | – | 5 & 2 | 3 & 1 | 5 & 1 | 6 & 1 | 4 & 6 | 6 & 1 | 6 & 1 | 4 & 1 | 6 & 3 | 6 & 3 | 6 & 2 | 3 & 2 |
| 19 | – | 3 & 1 | 6 & 4 | 2 & 1 | 6 & 1 | 4 & 1 | 6 & 5 | 6 & 1 | 6 & 5 | 4 & 6 | 4 & 1 | 4 & 1 | 4 & 4 |
| 20 | – | 6 & 4 | 5 & 3 | 5 & 4 | 6 & 1 | 4 & 4 | 6 & 2 | 4 & 2 | 1 & 1 | 6 & 1 | 1 & 1 | 6 & 1 | 6 & 3 |
| 21 | – | 4 & 1 | 6 & 3 | 6 & 6 | 6 & 2 | 6 & 4 | 4 & 2 | 2 & 2 | 5 & 2 | 6 & 6 | 6 & 6 | 6 & 2 | 6 & 1 |
| 22 | – | 6 & 6 | 6 & 4 | 5 & 5 | 3 & 1 | 6 & 4 | 3 & 3 | 3 & 3 | 5 & 1 | 2 & 1 | 4 & 3 | 5 & 2 | 3 & 1 |
| 23 | – | 6 & 6 | 6 & 4 | 5 & 2 | 3 & 1 | 6 & 6 | 5 & 4 | 6 & 6 | 5 & 2 | 5 & 4 | 3 & 1 | 4 & 2 | 4 & 4 |
| 24 | – | 4 & 2 | 4 & 6 | 6 & 1 | 4 & 2 | 5 & 5 | 6 & 4 | 6 & 4 | 6 & 2 | 3 & 2 | 3 & 1 | 4 & 2 | 6 & 2 |
| 25 | – | 2 & 2 | 5 & 2 | 5 & 3 | 4 & 3 | 5 & 4 | 6 & 4 | 2 & 1 | 6 & 2 | 6 & 6 | 3 & 1 | 6 & 1 | 6 & 1 |
| 26 | – | 6 & 1 | 6 & 1 | 5 & 1 | 5 & 1 | 4 & 4 | 5 & 3 | 5 & 1 | 5 & 1 | 4 & 3 | 5 & 1 | 6 & 3 | 6 & 1 |
| 27 | – | 6 & 4 | 5 & 4 | 3 & 3 | 6 & 4 | 5 & 4 | 5 & 2 | 3 & 2 | 5 & 2 | 5 & 3 | 5 & 3 | 6 & 5 | 2 & 1 |
| 28 | – | 3 & 2 | 3 & 1 | 6 & 6 | 3 & 3 | 3 & 2 | 3 & 2 | 6 & 3 | 6 & 3 | 4 & 1 | 5 & 2 | 4 & 1 | 5 & 4 |
| 29 | 5 & 3 | 4 & 1 | 6 & 2 | 6 & 3 | 4 & 2 | | 4 & 2 | 6 & 3 | 6 & 3 | 4 & 2 | 6 & 2 | 4 & 1 | – |
| 30 | 3 & 1 | 6 & 6 | 6 & 1 | 6 & 1 | 5 & 2 | | 5 & 5 | 6 & 2 | 6 & 3 | 6 & 3 | 5 & 2 | 6 & 1 | – |
| 31 | | 5 & 1 | | 1 & 1 | 4 & 3 | | 6 & 3 | | 5 & 1 | | 6 & 3 | 6 & 3 | |

159

Letters to On Kawara
365 Days
26 Oct. 2020 - 26 Oct. 2021

OCT 2020

| | |
|---|---|
| 01 | – |
| 02 | – |
| 03 | – |
| 04 | – |
| 05 | – |
| 06 | – |
| 07 | – |
| 08 | – |
| 09 | – |
| 10 | – |
| 11 | – |
| 12 | – |
| 13 | – |
| 14 | – |
| 15 | – |
| 16 | – |
| 17 | – |
| 18 | – |
| 19 | – |
| 20 | – |
| 21 | – |
| 22 | – |
| 23 | – |
| 24 | – |
| 25 | – |
| 26 | 099.90 |
| 27 | 098.90 |
| 28 | 098.90 |
| 29 | 100.90 |
| 30 | 098.90 |
| 31 | 096.90 |

NOV 2020

| 01 | 096.90 |
|----|--------|
| 02 | 096.90 |
| 03 | 096.90 |
| 04 | 096.90 |
| 05 | 097.90 |
| 06 | 097.90 |
| 07 | 098.90 |
| 08 | 098.90 |
| 09 | 097.90 |
| 10 | 097.90 |
| 11 | 099.90 |
| 12 | 101.90 |
| 13 | 100.90 |
| 14 | 099.90 |
| 15 | 098.90 |
| 16 | 098.90 |
| 17 | 098.90 |
| 18 | 098.90 |
| 19 | 098.90 |
| 20 | 098.90 |
| 21 | 099.90 |
| 22 | 099.90 |
| 23 | 099.90 |
| 24 | 099.90 |
| 25 | 101.90 |
| 26 | 103.90 |
| 27 | 104.90 |
| 28 | 104.90 |
| 29 | 104.90 |
| 30 | 103.90 |

DEC 2020

| | |
|---|---|
| 01 | 103.90 |
| 02 | 102.90 |
| 03 | 101.90 |
| 04 | 101.90 |
| 05 | 102.90 |
| 06 | 102.90 |
| 07 | 102.90 |
| 08 | 102.90 |
| 09 | 102.90 |
| 10 | 101.90 |
| 11 | 102.90 |
| 12 | 103.90 |
| 13 | 103.90 |
| 14 | 103.90 |
| 15 | 103.90 |
| 16 | 103.90 |
| 17 | 103.90 |
| 18 | 105.90 |
| 19 | 106.90 |
| 20 | 106.90 |
| 21 | 106.90 |
| 22 | 106.90 |
| 23 | 105.90 |
| 24 | 104.90 |
| 25 | 106.90 |
| 26 | 106.90 |
| 27 | 106.90 |
| 28 | 106.90 |
| 29 | 106.90 |
| 30 | 106.90 |
| 31 | 106.90 |

JAN 2021

| | |
|---|---|
| 01 | 107.90 |
| 02 | 107.90 |
| 03 | 106.90 |
| 04 | 107.90 |
| 05 | 107.90 |
| 06 | 106.90 |
| 07 | 109.90 |
| 08 | 109.90 |
| 09 | 110.90 |
| 10 | 112.90 |
| 11 | 112.90 |
| 12 | 112.90 |
| 13 | 111.90 |
| 14 | 112.90 |
| 15 | 112.90 |
| 16 | 112.90 |
| 17 | 111.90 |
| 18 | 111.90 |
| 19 | 111.90 |
| 20 | 111.90 |
| 21 | 112.90 |
| 22 | 111.90 |
| 23 | 111.90 |
| 24 | 111.90 |
| 25 | 112.90 |
| 26 | 112.90 |
| 27 | 113.90 |
| 28 | 113.90 |
| 29 | 113.90 |
| 30 | 114.90 |
| 31 | 113.90 |

FEB 2021

| | |
|---|---|
| 01 | 113.90 |
| 02 | 113.90 |
| 03 | 114.90 |
| 04 | 115.90 |
| 05 | 116.90 |
| 06 | 117.90 |
| 07 | 117.90 |
| 08 | 117.90 |
| 09 | 117.90 |
| 10 | 117.90 |
| 11 | 117.90 |
| 12 | 116.90 |
| 13 | 116.90 |
| 14 | 117.90 |
| 15 | 117.90 |
| 16 | 117.90 |
| 17 | 117.90 |
| 18 | 120.90 |
| 19 | 122.90 |
| 20 | 121.90 |
| 21 | 121.90 |
| 22 | 121.90 |
| 23 | 121.90 |
| 24 | 122.90 |
| 25 | 123.90 |
| 26 | 124.90 |
| 27 | 124.90 |
| 28 | 124.90 |

MAR 2021

| | |
|---|---|
| 01 | 124.90 |
| 02 | 124.90 |
| 03 | 124.90 |
| 04 | 123.90 |
| 05 | 122.90 |
| 06 | 123.90 |
| 07 | 126.90 |
| 08 | 126.90 |
| 09 | 126.90 |
| 10 | 125.90 |
| 11 | 125.90 |
| 12 | 126.90 |
| 13 | 128.90 |
| 14 | 128.90 |
| 15 | 128.90 |
| 16 | 128.90 |
| 17 | 126.90 |
| 18 | 126.90 |
| 19 | 124.90 |
| 20 | 120.90 |
| 21 | 120.90 |
| 22 | 120.90 |
| 23 | 120.90 |
| 24 | 121.90 |
| 25 | 119.90 |
| 26 | 122.90 |
| 27 | 120.90 |
| 28 | 121.90 |
| 29 | 121.90 |
| 30 | 121.90 |
| 31 | 122.90 |

APR 2021

| | |
|---|---|
| 01 | 125.90 |
| 02 | 123.90 |
| 03 | 126.90 |
| 04 | 126.90 |
| 05 | 126.90 |
| 06 | 126.90 |
| 07 | 123.90 |
| 08 | 123.90 |
| 09 | 122.90 |
| 10 | 122.90 |
| 11 | 121.90 |
| 12 | 121.90 |
| 13 | 122.90 |
| 14 | 122.90 |
| 15 | 122.90 |
| 16 | 124.90 |
| 17 | 125.90 |
| 18 | 129.90 |
| 19 | 129.90 |
| 20 | 129.90 |
| 21 | 130.90 |
| 22 | 129.90 |
| 23 | 127.90 |
| 24 | 127.90 |
| 25 | 127.90 |
| 26 | 127.90 |
| 27 | 127.90 |
| 28 | 126.90 |
| 29 | 129.90 |
| 30 | 131.90 |

MAY 2021

| | |
|----|--------|
| 01 | 131.90 |
| 02 | 129.90 |
| 03 | 129.90 |
| 04 | 129.90 |
| 05 | 130.90 |
| 06 | 133.90 |
| 07 | 132.90 |
| 08 | 130.90 |
| 09 | 130.90 |
| 10 | 130.90 |
| 11 | 130.90 |
| 12 | 130.90 |
| 13 | 130.90 |
| 14 | 131.90 |
| 15 | 129.90 |
| 16 | 130.90 |
| 17 | 130.90 |
| 18 | 130.90 |
| 19 | 131.90 |
| 20 | 131.90 |
| 21 | 129.90 |
| 22 | 127.90 |
| 23 | 127.90 |
| 24 | 128.90 |
| 25 | 128.90 |
| 26 | 128.90 |
| 27 | 129.90 |
| 28 | 131.90 |
| 29 | 131.90 |
| 30 | 130.90 |
| 31 | 130.90 |

JUN 2021

| | |
|---|---|
| 01 | 130.90 |
| 02 | 130.90 |
| 03 | 131.90 |
| 04 | 132.90 |
| 05 | 133.90 |
| 06 | 133.90 |
| 07 | 133.90 |
| 08 | 133.90 |
| 09 | 132.90 |
| 10 | 133.90 |
| 11 | 133.90 |
| 12 | 133.90 |
| 13 | 132.90 |
| 14 | 132.90 |
| 15 | 132.90 |
| 16 | 132.90 |
| 17 | 132.90 |
| 18 | 131.90 |
| 19 | 131.90 |
| 20 | 132.90 |
| 21 | 132.90 |
| 22 | 132.90 |
| 23 | 132.90 |
| 24 | 133.90 |
| 25 | 135.90 |
| 26 | 136.90 |
| 27 | 135.90 |
| 28 | 135.90 |
| 29 | 135.90 |
| 30 | 133.90 |

JUL 2021

| | |
|---|---|
| 01 | 134.90 |
| 02 | 135.90 |
| 03 | 135.90 |
| 04 | 136.90 |
| 05 | 136.90 |
| 06 | 136.90 |
| 07 | 136.90 |
| 08 | 134.90 |
| 09 | 134.90 |
| 10 | 136.90 |
| 11 | 137.90 |
| 12 | 137.90 |
| 13 | 137.90 |
| 14 | 136.90 |
| 15 | 138.90 |
| 16 | 137.90 |
| 17 | 136.90 |
| 18 | 136.90 |
| 19 | 136.90 |
| 20 | 136.90 |
| 21 | 132.90 |
| 22 | 132.90 |
| 23 | 135.90 |
| 24 | 137.90 |
| 25 | 138.90 |
| 26 | 138.90 |
| 27 | 138.90 |
| 28 | 138.90 |
| 29 | 139.90 |
| 30 | 138.90 |
| 31 | 139.90 |

AUG 2021

| 01 | 140.90 |
|----|--------|
| 02 | 140.90 |
| 03 | 140.90 |
| 04 | 140.90 |
| 05 | 138.90 |
| 06 | 138.90 |
| 07 | 139.90 |
| 08 | 138.90 |
| 09 | 138.90 |
| 10 | 138.90 |
| 11 | 138.90 |
| 12 | 138.90 |
| 13 | 140.90 |
| 14 | 139.90 |
| 15 | 138.90 |
| 16 | 138.90 |
| 17 | 138.90 |
| 18 | 136.90 |
| 19 | 135.90 |
| 20 | 134.90 |
| 21 | 133.90 |
| 22 | 132.90 |
| 23 | 132.90 |
| 24 | 132.90 |
| 25 | 134.90 |
| 26 | 135.90 |
| 27 | 140.90 |
| 28 | 138.90 |
| 29 | 138.90 |
| 30 | 138.90 |
| 31 | 138.90 |

SEP 2021

| | |
|---|---|
| 01 | 141.90 |
| 02 | 140.90 |
| 03 | 138.90 |
| 04 | 140.90 |
| 05 | 138.90 |
| 06 | 138.90 |
| 07 | 138.90 |
| 08 | 138.90 |
| 09 | 138.90 |
| 10 | 139.90 |
| 11 | 138.90 |
| 12 | 139.90 |
| 13 | 139.90 |
| 14 | 139.90 |
| 15 | 138.90 |
| 16 | 138.90 |
| 17 | 140.90 |
| 18 | 138.90 |
| 19 | 137.90 |
| 20 | 137.90 |
| 21 | 137.90 |
| 22 | 135.90 |
| 23 | 136.90 |
| 24 | 135.90 |
| 25 | 137.90 |
| 26 | 136.90 |
| 27 | 136.90 |
| 28 | 136.90 |
| 29 | 137.90 |
| 30 | 136.90 |

OCT 2021

| | |
|----|--------|
| 01 | 137.90 |
| 02 | 139.90 |
| 03 | 139.90 |
| 04 | 140.90 |
| 05 | 140.90 |
| 06 | 142.90 |
| 07 | 144.90 |
| 08 | 142.90 |
| 09 | 143.90 |
| 10 | 144.90 |
| 11 | 144.90 |
| 12 | 144.90 |
| 13 | 144.90 |
| 14 | 144.90 |
| 15 | 145.90 |
| 16 | 146.90 |
| 17 | 148.90 |
| 18 | 148.90 |
| 19 | 148.90 |
| 20 | 148.90 |
| 21 | 148.90 |
| 22 | 149.90 |
| 23 | 148.90 |
| 24 | 148.90 |
| 25 | 148.90 |
| 26 | – |
| 27 | – |
| 28 | – |
| 29 | – |
| 30 | – |
| 31 | – |

Notes:

Observing & Recording GAS price
At Esso Gas Station (Bayview & Sheppard / Toronto)

26 Oct. 2020 – 26 Oct. 2021

096.90 (L)
149.90 (H)

208.90 (Today May 18, 2022)

—

| OCT 2020 | NOV 2020 | DEC 2020 | JAN 2021 | FEB 2021 | MAR 2021 | APR 2021 | MAY 2021 | JUN 2021 | JUL 2021 | AUG 2021 | SEP 2021 | OCT 2021 |
|---|---|---|---|---|---|---|---|---|---|---|---|---|
| 01 – | 01 096.90 | 01 103.90 | 01 107.90 | 01 113.90 | 01 124.90 | 01 125.90 | 01 131.90 | 01 130.90 | 01 134.90 | 01 140.90 | 01 141.90 | 01 137.90 |
| 02 – | 02 096.90 | 02 102.90 | 02 107.90 | 02 113.90 | 02 124.90 | 02 123.90 | 02 129.90 | 02 130.90 | 02 135.90 | 02 140.90 | 02 140.90 | 02 139.90 |
| 03 – | 03 096.90 | 03 101.90 | 03 106.90 | 03 114.90 | 03 124.90 | 03 126.90 | 03 129.90 | 03 131.90 | 03 135.90 | 03 140.90 | 03 138.90 | 03 139.90 |
| 04 – | 04 096.90 | 04 101.90 | 04 107.90 | 04 115.90 | 04 123.90 | 04 126.90 | 04 129.90 | 04 132.90 | 04 136.90 | 04 140.90 | 04 140.90 | 04 140.90 |
| 05 – | 05 097.90 | 05 102.90 | 05 107.90 | 05 116.90 | 05 122.90 | 05 126.90 | 05 130.90 | 05 133.90 | 05 136.90 | 05 138.90 | 05 138.90 | 05 140.90 |
| 06 – | 06 097.90 | 06 102.90 | 06 106.90 | 06 117.90 | 06 123.90 | 06 126.90 | 06 133.90 | 06 133.90 | 06 136.90 | 06 138.90 | 06 138.90 | 06 142.90 |
| 07 – | 07 098.90 | 07 102.90 | 07 109.90 | 07 117.90 | 07 126.90 | 07 123.90 | 07 132.90 | 07 133.90 | 07 136.90 | 07 139.90 | 07 138.90 | 07 144.90 |
| 08 – | 08 098.90 | 08 102.90 | 08 109.90 | 08 117.90 | 08 126.90 | 08 123.90 | 08 130.90 | 08 133.90 | 08 134.90 | 08 138.90 | 08 138.90 | 08 142.90 |
| 09 – | 09 097.90 | 09 102.90 | 09 110.90 | 09 117.90 | 09 126.90 | 09 122.90 | 09 132.90 | 09 132.90 | 09 134.90 | 09 138.90 | 09 138.90 | 09 143.90 |
| 10 – | 10 097.90 | 10 101.90 | 10 112.90 | 10 117.90 | 10 125.90 | 10 122.90 | 10 130.90 | 10 133.90 | 10 134.90 | 10 138.90 | 10 139.90 | 10 144.90 |
| 11 – | 11 099.90 | 11 102.90 | 11 112.90 | 11 117.90 | 11 125.90 | 11 121.90 | 11 130.90 | 11 133.90 | 11 137.90 | 11 138.90 | 11 138.90 | 11 144.90 |
| 12 – | 12 101.90 | 12 103.90 | 12 112.90 | 12 116.90 | 12 126.90 | 12 121.90 | 12 130.90 | 12 133.90 | 12 137.90 | 12 138.90 | 12 139.90 | 12 144.90 |
| 13 – | 13 100.90 | 13 103.90 | 13 111.90 | 13 116.90 | 13 128.90 | 13 122.90 | 13 130.90 | 13 132.90 | 13 137.90 | 13 140.90 | 13 139.90 | 13 144.90 |
| 14 – | 14 099.90 | 14 103.90 | 14 112.90 | 14 117.90 | 14 128.90 | 14 122.90 | 14 131.90 | 14 132.90 | 14 136.90 | 14 139.90 | 14 139.90 | 14 144.90 |
| 15 – | 15 098.90 | 15 103.90 | 15 112.90 | 15 117.90 | 15 128.90 | 15 122.90 | 15 129.90 | 15 132.90 | 15 138.90 | 15 138.90 | 15 138.90 | 15 145.90 |
| 16 – | 16 098.90 | 16 103.90 | 16 112.90 | 16 117.90 | 16 128.90 | 16 124.90 | 16 130.90 | 16 132.90 | 16 137.90 | 16 138.90 | 16 138.90 | 16 146.90 |
| 17 – | 17 098.90 | 17 103.90 | 17 111.90 | 17 117.90 | 17 126.90 | 17 125.90 | 17 130.90 | 17 132.90 | 17 136.90 | 17 138.90 | 17 140.90 | 17 148.90 |
| 18 – | 18 098.90 | 18 105.90 | 18 111.90 | 18 120.90 | 18 126.90 | 18 129.90 | 18 130.90 | 18 131.90 | 18 136.90 | 18 136.90 | 18 138.90 | 18 148.90 |
| 19 – | 19 098.90 | 19 106.90 | 19 111.90 | 19 122.90 | 19 124.90 | 19 129.90 | 19 131.90 | 19 131.90 | 19 136.90 | 19 135.90 | 19 137.90 | 19 148.90 |
| 20 – | 20 098.90 | 20 106.90 | 20 111.90 | 20 121.90 | 20 120.90 | 20 129.90 | 20 131.90 | 20 132.90 | 20 136.90 | 20 134.90 | 20 137.90 | 20 148.90 |
| 21 – | 21 099.90 | 21 106.90 | 21 112.90 | 21 121.90 | 21 120.90 | 21 130.90 | 21 129.90 | 21 132.90 | 21 133.90 | 21 133.90 | 21 137.90 | 21 148.90 |
| 22 – | 22 099.90 | 22 106.90 | 22 111.90 | 22 121.90 | 22 120.90 | 22 129.90 | 22 127.90 | 22 132.90 | 22 132.90 | 22 132.90 | 22 135.90 | 22 149.90 |
| 23 – | 23 099.90 | 23 105.90 | 23 111.90 | 23 121.90 | 23 120.90 | 23 127.90 | 23 127.90 | 23 132.90 | 23 135.90 | 23 136.90 | 23 136.90 | 23 148.90 |
| 24 – | 24 099.90 | 24 104.90 | 24 111.90 | 24 122.90 | 24 121.90 | 24 127.90 | 24 128.90 | 24 133.90 | 24 137.90 | 24 132.90 | 24 135.90 | 24 148.90 |
| 25 – | 25 101.90 | 25 106.90 | 25 112.90 | 25 123.90 | 25 119.90 | 25 127.90 | 25 128.90 | 25 135.90 | 25 138.90 | 25 134.90 | 25 137.90 | 25 – |
| 26 099.90 | 26 103.90 | 26 106.90 | 26 112.90 | 26 124.90 | 26 122.90 | 26 127.90 | 26 128.90 | 26 135.90 | 26 138.90 | 26 135.90 | 26 136.90 | 26 – |
| 27 098.90 | 27 104.90 | 27 106.90 | 27 113.90 | 27 124.90 | 27 120.90 | 27 127.90 | 27 129.90 | 27 135.90 | 27 138.90 | 27 140.90 | 27 136.90 | 27 – |
| 28 098.90 | 28 104.90 | 28 106.90 | 28 113.90 | 28 124.90 | 28 121.90 | 28 129.90 | 28 131.90 | 28 135.90 | 28 138.90 | 28 138.90 | 28 136.90 | 28 – |
| 29 100.90 | 29 104.90 | 29 106.90 | 29 113.90 | | 29 121.90 | 29 129.90 | 29 131.90 | 29 135.90 | 29 139.90 | 29 139.90 | 29 137.90 | 29 – |
| 30 098.90 | 30 103.90 | 30 106.90 | 30 114.90 | | 30 121.90 | 30 131.90 | 30 131.90 | 30 133.90 | 30 136.90 | 30 138.90 | 30 136.90 | 30 – |
| 31 096.90 | | 31 106.90 | 31 113.90 | | 31 122.90 | | 31 130.90 | | 31 139.90 | 31 138.90 | | 31 – |

9 Letters To <u>Hiroshi Sugimoto</u>
Seascapes 1980 – 2002
October 2021

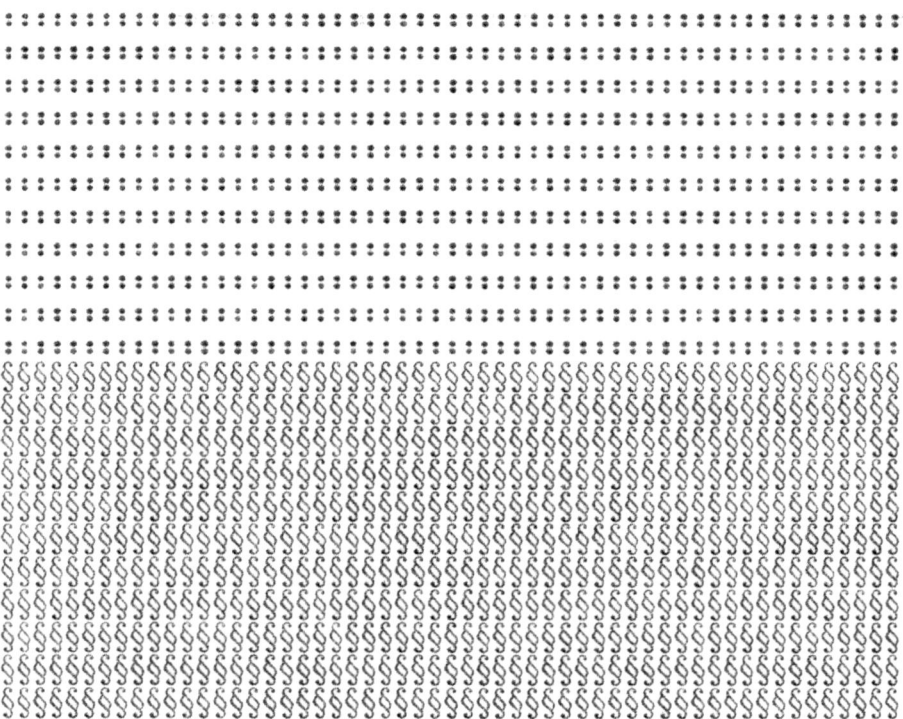

```
++++++++++++++++++++++++++++++++++++++++++++++++++++++++++++
++++++++++++++++++++++++++++++++++++++++++++++++++++++++++++
++++++++++++++++++++++++++++++++++++++++++++++++++++++++++++
++++++++++++++++++++++++++++++++++++++++++++++++++++++++++++
++++++++++++++++++++++++++++++++++++++++++++++++++++++++++++
++++++++++++++++++++++++++++++++++++++++++++++++++++++++++++
++++++++++++++++++++++++++++++++++++++++++++++++++++++++++++
++++++++++++++++++++++++++++++++++++++++++++++++++++++++++++
++++++++++++++++++++++++++++++++++++++++++++++++++++++++++++
++++++++++++++++++++++++++++++++++++++++++++++++++++++++++++
++++++++++++++++++++++++++++++++++++++++++++++++++++++++++++
============================================================
============================================================
============================================================
============================================================
============================================================
============================================================
============================================================
============================================================
============================================================
============================================================
```

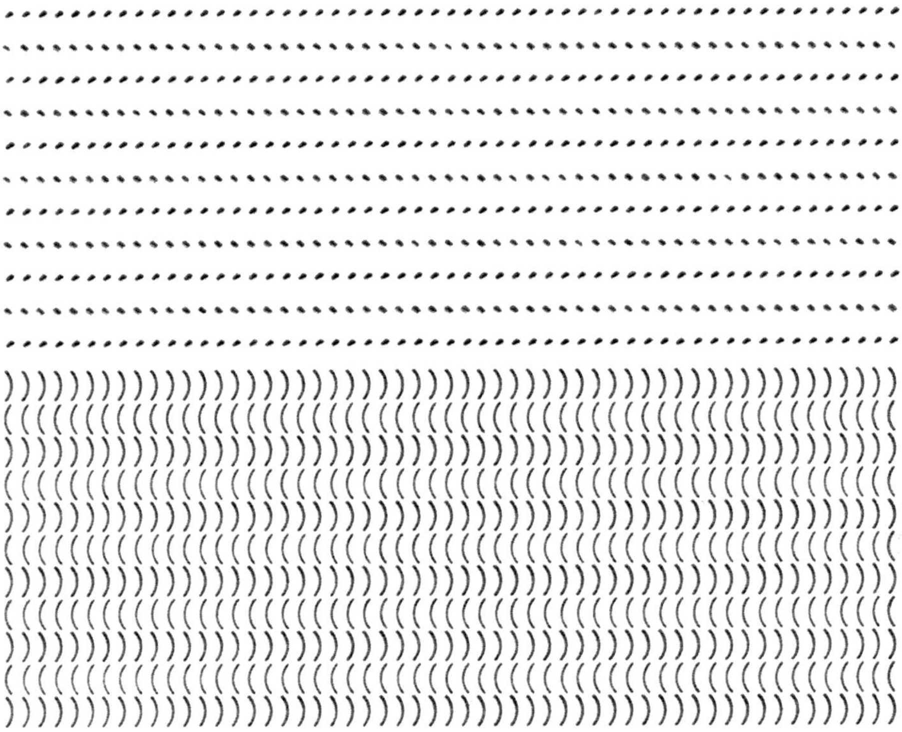

'' '' '' '' '' '' '' '' '' '' '' '' '' '' '' '' '' '' '' '' '' '' '' '' '' '' '' '' '' '' '' '' '' '' '' '' '' '' '' '' '' '' '' '' '' '' '' '' ''
'' '' '' '' '' '' '' '' '' '' '' '' '' '' '' '' '' '' '' '' '' '' '' '' '' '' '' '' '' '' '' '' '' '' '' '' '' '' '' '' '' '' '' '' '' '' '' '' ''
'' '' '' '' '' '' '' '' '' '' '' '' '' '' '' '' '' '' '' '' '' '' '' '' '' '' '' '' '' '' '' '' '' '' '' '' '' '' '' '' '' '' '' '' '' '' '' '' ''
'' '' '' '' '' '' '' '' '' '' '' '' '' '' '' '' '' '' '' '' '' '' '' '' '' '' '' '' '' '' '' '' '' '' '' '' '' '' '' '' '' '' '' '' '' '' '' '' ''
'' '' '' '' '' '' '' '' '' '' '' '' '' '' '' '' '' '' '' '' '' '' '' '' '' '' '' '' '' '' '' '' '' '' '' '' '' '' '' '' '' '' '' '' '' '' '' '' ''
'' '' '' '' '' '' '' '' '' '' '' '' '' '' '' '' '' '' '' '' '' '' '' '' '' '' '' '' '' '' '' '' '' '' '' '' '' '' '' '' '' '' '' '' '' '' '' '' ''
'' '' '' '' '' '' '' '' '' '' '' '' '' '' '' '' '' '' '' '' '' '' '' '' '' '' '' '' '' '' '' '' '' '' '' '' '' '' '' '' '' '' '' '' '' '' '' '' ''
'' '' '' '' '' '' '' '' '' '' '' '' '' '' '' '' '' '' '' '' '' '' '' '' '' '' '' '' '' '' '' '' '' '' '' '' '' '' '' '' '' '' '' '' '' '' '' '' ''
'' '' '' '' '' '' '' '' '' '' '' '' '' '' '' '' '' '' '' '' '' '' '' '' '' '' '' '' '' '' '' '' '' '' '' '' '' '' '' '' '' '' '' '' '' '' '' '' ''
'' '' '' '' '' '' '' '' '' '' '' '' '' '' '' '' '' '' '' '' '' '' '' '' '' '' '' '' '' '' '' '' '' '' '' '' '' '' '' '' '' '' '' '' '' '' '' '' ''
'' '' '' '' '' '' '' '' '' '' '' '' '' '' '' '' '' '' '' '' '' '' '' '' '' '' '' '' '' '' '' '' '' '' '' '' '' '' '' '' '' '' '' '' '' '' '' '' ''
222222222222222222222222222222222222222222222222222
222222222222222222222222222222222222222222222222222
222222222222222222222222222222222222222222222222222
222222222222222222222222222222222222222222222222222
222222222222222222222222222222222222222222222222222
222222222222222222222222222222222222222222222222222
222222222222222222222222222222222222222222222222222
222222222222222222222222222222222222222222222222222
222222222222222222222222222222222222222222222222222
222222222222222222222222222222222222222222222222222
222222222222222222222222222222222222222222222222222

189

Letter to Georges Perec
31 Jan.   2022

A one-month diet in alphabetical order:
attempt at an inventory of the liquid and solid foodstuffs
ingurgitated by me in the course of an artist residency
in Gushul Studio, Blairmore, Crowsnest Pass, AB. Canada

# List A

| Item | Quantity |
|---|---|
| Apple Pie | 1 piece |
| Bacon | 3 stripes |
| Bagel | 30 |
| Banana | 16 |
| Beef Pie | 1 |
| Beef Sausage | 6 |
| Berries (mixed) | 250 gr. |
| Biscotti | 500 gr. |
| Black Berry | 170 gr. |
| Black Peppercorn | 35 gr. |
| Blue Berry | 250 gr. |
| Borscht (Polish Beet Soup) | 1 |
| Cheesecake | 1 |
| Chicken Brest | 10 slices |
| Chicken Stew (Sir-Nardoon) | 1 |
| Chocolate | |
|     KitKat | 3 bars |
|     Lindt | 1 bar |
|     Ritter Sport | 2 bars |
| Ciabatta Bun | 8 |
| Corned Beef | 10 slices |
| Cream Cheese | 3 packs, 230 gr. each |
| Croissant (ham & cheese) | 1 |
| Cucumber | 1 |
| Digestive | 2 packs, 750 gr. each |
| Egg (brown) | 24 |
| Eggs Benedict | 2 |
| Fries | |
|     Home Fries | 2 |
|     French Fries | 1 |
|     Sweet Potato Fries | 2 |
| Fruit Salad (mixed) | 2 bowls, 350 gr. each |
| Ginger Root | 1 |
| Green Onion | 2 bunches |
| Ice-cream | 1 |
| Kiwi | 6 |

| | |
|---|---|
| Mushroom (white) | $\frac{7}{200}$ gr. |
| Mustard (dijon) | $\frac{200}{700}$ gr. |
| Nuts (mixed) | $\frac{700}{1}$ gr. |
| Pastie (sausage roll) | $\frac{1}{10}$ slices |
| Pastrami | $\frac{10}{20}$ slices |
| Pear (red) | $\frac{20}{500}$ gr. |
| Peanut Butter | $\frac{500}{15}$ gr. |
| Pierogi | $\underline{15}$ |
| Pizza | |
|     Deluxe | $\frac{1}{1}$ |
|     Italian Easter | $\frac{1}{1}$ |
|     All Veg | $\frac{1}{1}$ |
| Samosa | $\underline{1}$ |
| Sandwich | |
|     Bison Burger | $\frac{2}{1}$ |
|     Bologna | $\frac{1}{2}$ |
|     Ham & Cheese | $\frac{2}{2}$ |
|     Turkey & Havarti | $\frac{2}{1}$ |
| Soup | $\underline{1}$ |
| Steak | |
|     T-Bone | $\frac{1}{2}$ |
|     Tenderloin | $\frac{2}{3}$ |
|     Top Sirloin | $\frac{3}{1}$ |
|     Tuna | $\frac{1}{4}$ |
| Sweet Bell Pepper | $\frac{4}{10}$ slices |
| Swiss Cheese | 10 slices |
| Toast | 2 slices |
| Turkey (oven roasted) | 10 slices |
| Yellow Fin Tuna Sashimi | $\frac{1}{8}$ |
| Yogurt Bowl (granola & berries) | $\frac{1}{8}$ |

List B .

| | |
|---|---|
| Absinthe | 3 oz |
| Beer | |
|     Czech Dark Lager | 5 oz |
|     IPA | 1 pt. |
|     Irish Red Ale | 10 oz |
|     Keith's Red | 1 pt. |
|     Pastry Stout | 10 oz |
|     Whiskey Six | 5 oz |
| Cognac (Hennessy) | 750 ml |
| Grand Marnier | 3 oz |
| Krupnik | 5 oz |
| Vodka | 20 oz |
| Whisky (Glenlivet) | 5 oz |

List C .

| | |
|---|---|
| Coffee | 2 |
| Espresso | 53 (d) |
| Mineral Water (Eska) | 2 bottles, 600 ml |
| Water | 75 L (300 glasses) |

Letter to <u>Christo and Jeanne-Claude</u>
14 Feb.   2022

C§J C§J C§J C§J C§J C§J C§J C§J C§J C§J C§J C§J C§J
C§J C§J C§J C§J C§J C§J C§J C§J C§J C§J C§J C§J C§J
C§J C§J C§J C§J C§J C§J C§J C§J C§J C§J C§J C§J C§J
C§J C§J C§J C§J C§J C§J C§J C§J C§J C§J C§J C§J C§J
C§J C§J C§J C§J C§J C§J C§J C§J C§J C§J C§J C§J C§J
C§J C§J C§J C§J C§J C§J C§J C§J C§J C§J C§J C§J C§J
C§J C§J C§J C§J C§J C§J C§J C§J C§J C§J C§J C§J C§J
C§J C§J C§J C§J C§J C§J C§J C§J C§J C§J C§J C§J C§J
C§J C§J C§J C§J C§J C§J C§J C§J C§J C§J C§J C§J C§J
C§J C§J C§J C§J C§J C§J C§J C§J C§J C§J C§J C§J C§J
C§J C§J C§J C§J C§J C§J C§J C§J C§J C§J C§J C§J C§J
C§J C§J C§J C§J C§J C§J C§J C§J C§J C§J C§J C§J C§J
C§J C§J C§J C§J C§J C§J C§J C§J C§J C§J C§J C§J C§J
C§J C§J C§J C§J C§J C§J C§J C§J C§J C§J C§J C§J C§J
C§J C§J C§J C§J C§J C§J C§J C§J C§J C§J C§J C§J C§J
C§J C§J C§J C§J C§J C§J C§J C§J C§J C§J C§J C§J C§J
C§J C§J C§J C§J C§J C§J C§J C§J C§J C§J C§J C§J C§J
C§J C§J C§J C§J C§J C§J C§J C§J C§J C§J C§J C§J C§J
C§J C§J C§J C§J C§J C§J C§J C§J C§J C§J C§J C§J C§J
C§J C§J C§J C§J C§J C§J C§J C§J C§J C§J C§J C§J C§J
C§J C§J C§J C§J C§J C§J C§J C§J C§J C§J C§J C§J C§J
C§J C§J C§J C§J C§J C§J C§J C§J C§J C§J C§J C§J C§J
C§J C§J C§J C§J C§J C§J C§J C§J C§J C§J C§J C§J C§J
C§J C§J C§J C§J C§J C§J C§J C§J C§J C§J C§J C§J C§J
C§J C§J C§J C§J C§J C§J C§J C§J C§J C§J C§J C§J C§J

527

Letter to Carlos Cruz - Diez
16 Mar.   2022

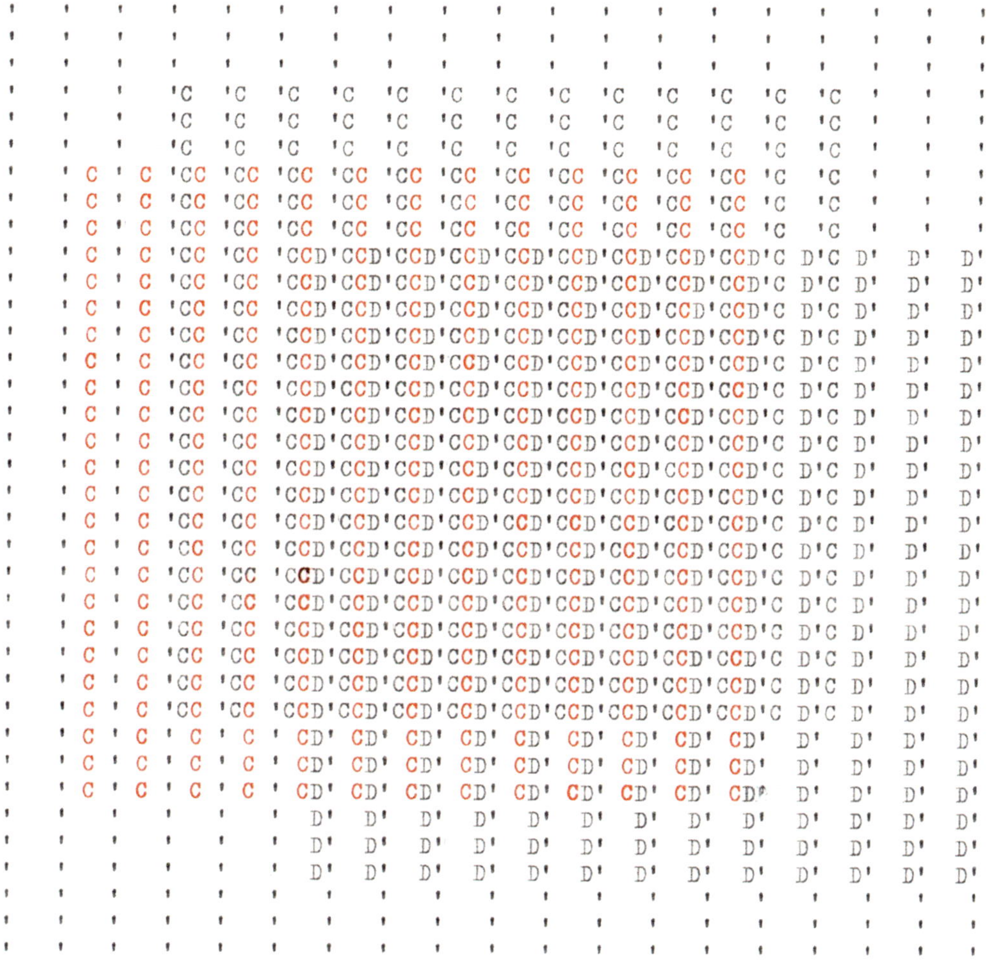

5 Letters to <u>Max Cole</u>
17 Mar. 2022

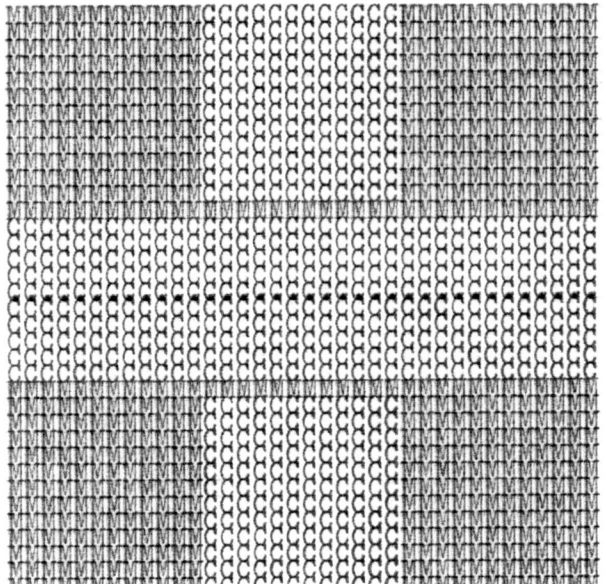

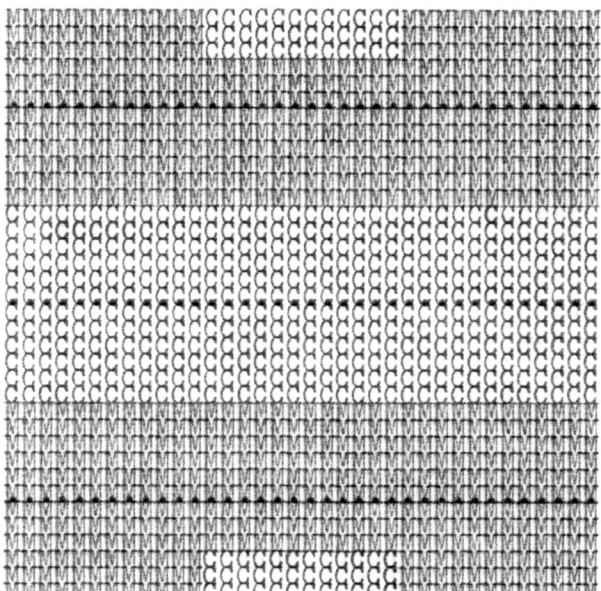

205

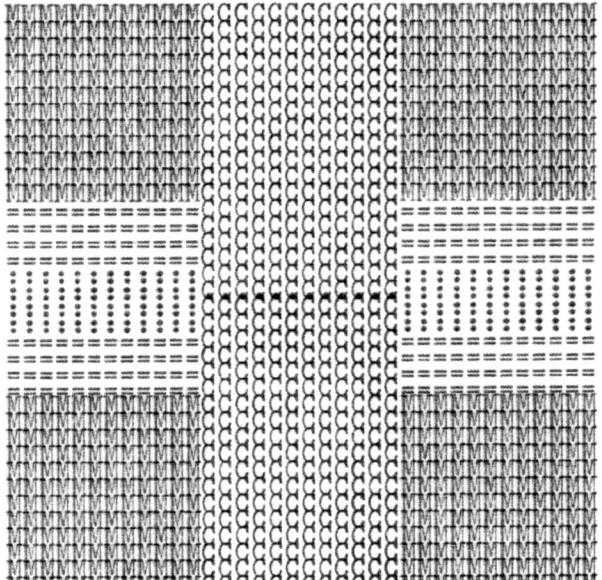

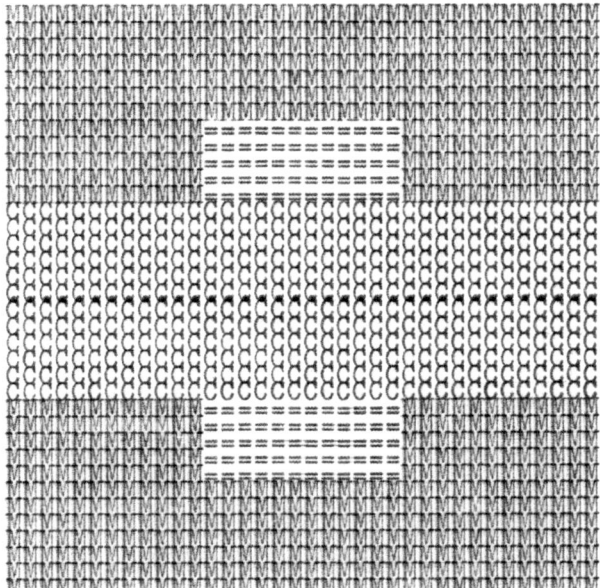

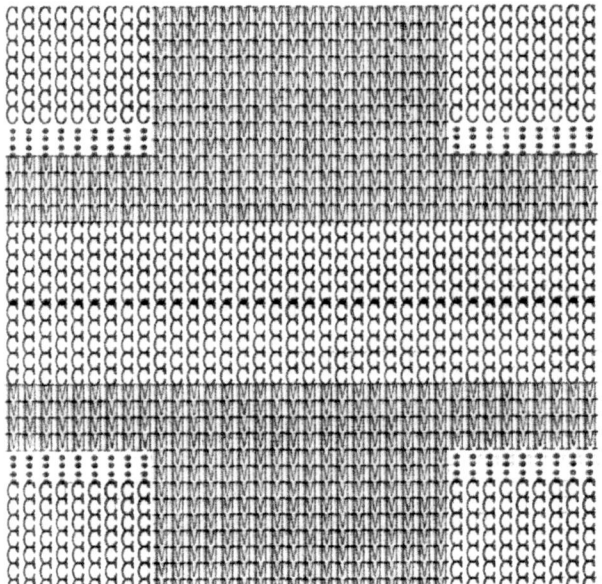

Letter to <u>Ai Weiwei</u>
Mar. 23   2022

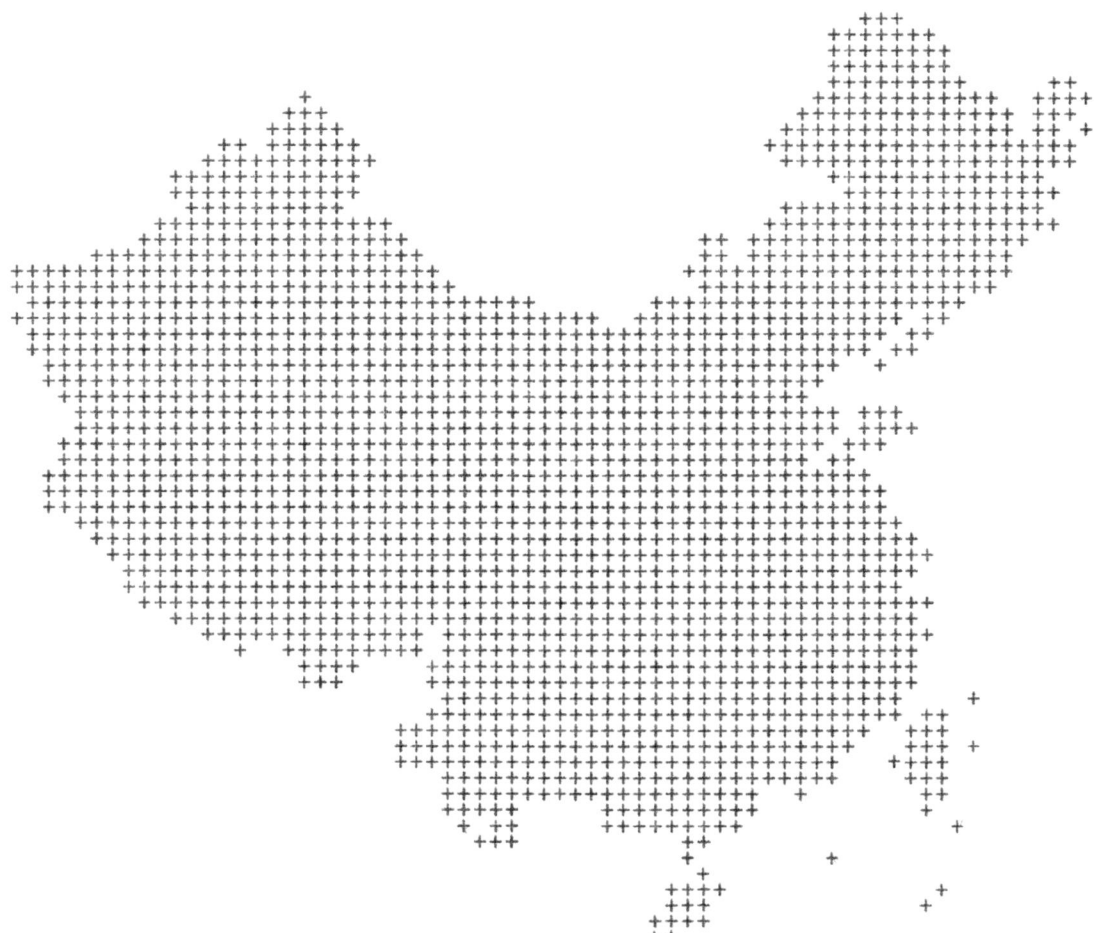

211

1000 Letters to Phi (Ø)
23 Mar. 2022

```
1.6180339887 4989484820 4586834365 6381177203 0917980576
  2862135448 6227052604 6281890244 9707207204 1893911374
  8475408807 5386891752 1266338622 2353693179 3180060766
  7263544333 8908659593 9582905638 3226613199 2829026788
  0675208766 8925017116 9620703222 1043216269 5486262963
  1361443814 9758701220 3408058879 5445474924 6185695364
  8644492410 4432077134 4947049565 8467885098 7433944221
  2544877066 4780915884 6074998871 2400765217 0575179788
  3416625624 9407589069 7040002812 1042762177 1117778053
  1531714101 1704666599 1466979873 1761356006 7087480710
  1317952368 9427521948 4353056783 0022878569 9782977834
  7845878228 9110976250 0302696156 1700250464 3382437764
  8610283831 2683303724 2926752631 1653392473 1671112115
  8818638513 3162038400 5222165791 2866752946 5490681131
  7159934323 5973494985 0904094762 1322298101 7261070596
  1164562990 9816290555 2085247903 5240602017 2799747175
  3427775927 7862561943 2082750513 1218156285 5122248093
  9471234145 1702237358 0577278616 0086883829 5230459264
  7878017889 9219902707 7690389532 1968198615 1437803149
  9741106926 0886742962 2675756052 3172777520 3536139362
  ...

TBC
```

3 Letters to <u>Gordon Matta-Clark</u>
30 Mar. 2022

What
I
do
to
buildings
is
what
some
do
with
languages
and
others
with
group
of
people
:
I
organize
them
in
order
to
explain
and
defend
the
need
for
change
.

Undoing
is
just
as
much
a
democratic
right
as
doing

.

Here
is
what
we
have
to
offer
you
in
its
most
elaborate
form
—
confusion
guided
by
a
clear
sense
of
purpose
.

Letter to <u>Mario Botta</u>
06 Apr.    2022

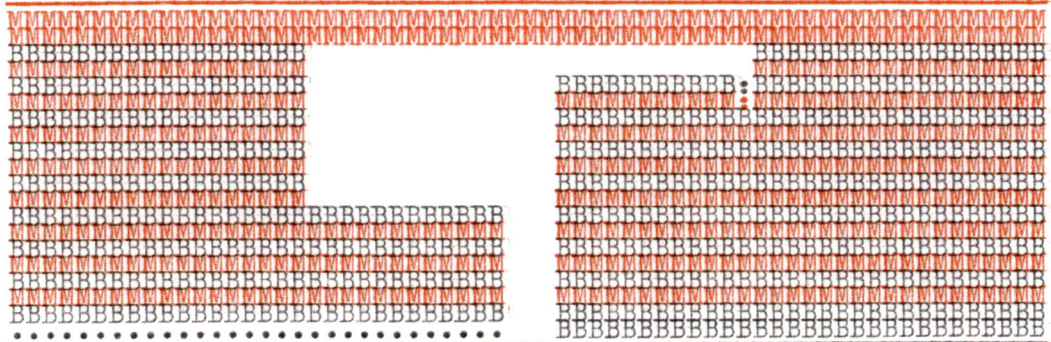

M.B

Letter to <u>Tadao Ando</u>
06 Apr.    2022

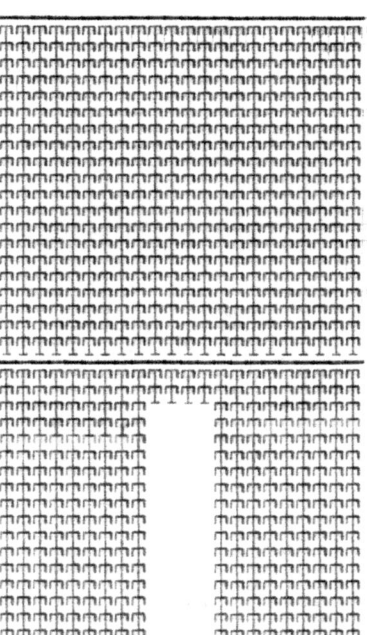

Letter to <u>Le Corbusier</u>
06 Apr.    2022

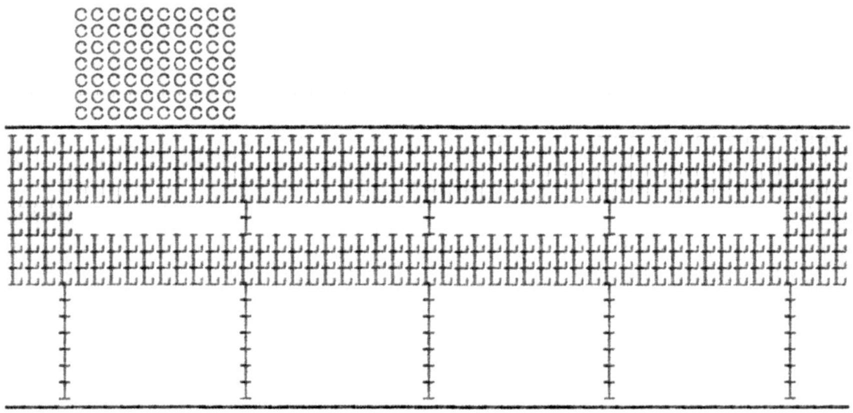

Letter to <u>Aldo Rossi</u>
06 Apr.    2022

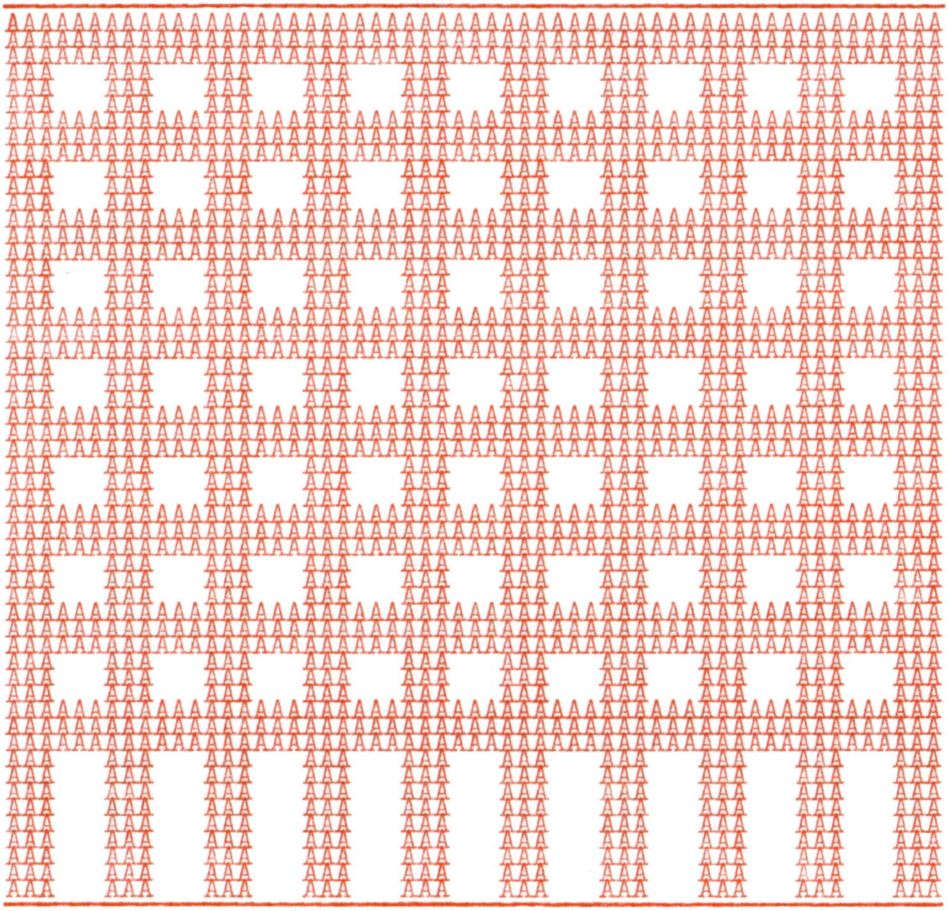

Letter to <u>Sol LeWitt</u>
13 Apr.   2022

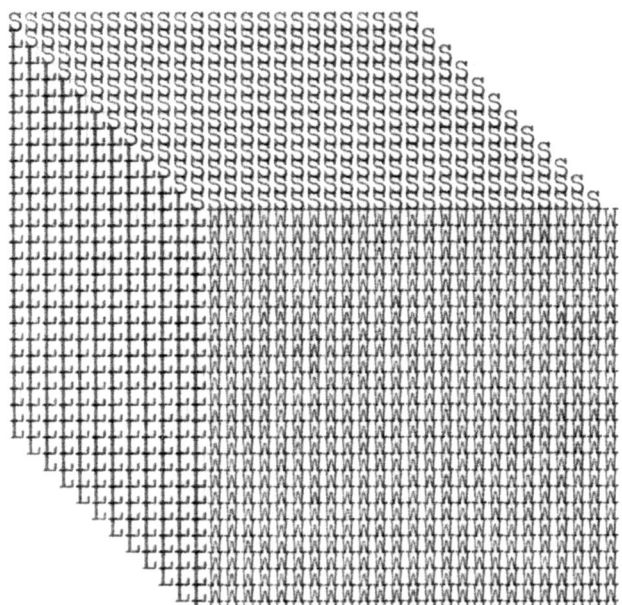

Letters to <u>Massimo Vignelli</u>
13 Apr.    2022

| M | T | W | T | F | S | S |
|---|---|---|---|---|---|---|
|   |   |   |   | 1 | 2 | 3 |
| 4 | 5 | 6 | 7 | 8 | 9 | 10 |
| 11 | 12 | 13 | 14 | 15 | 16 | 17 |
| 18 | 19 | 20 | 21 | 22 | 23 | 24 |
| 25 | 26 | 27 | 28 | 29 | 30 |   |

2022    April

Garamond, 1532
ABCDEFGHIJKLMNOPQRSTUVWXYZ
abcdefghijklmnopqrstuvwxyz
1234567890

Bodoni, 1788
ABCDEFGHIJKLMNOPQRSTUVWXYZ
abcdefghijklmnopqrstuvwxyz
1234567890

Century Expanded, 1900
ABCDEFGHIJKLMNOPQRSTUVWXYZ
abcdefghijklmnopqrstuvwxyz
1234567890

Futura, 1930
ABCDEFGHIJKLMNOPQRSTUVWXYZ
abcdefghijklmnopqrstuvwxyz

Times Roman, 1931
ABCDEFGHIJKLMNOPQRSTUVWXYZ
abcdefghijklmnopqrstuvwxyz
1234567890

Helvetica, 1957
ABCDEFGHIJKLMNOPQRSTUVWXYZ
abcdefghijklmnopqrstuvwxyz
1234567890

:)

233

GRID : GRID : GRID : GRID : GRID : GRID
GRID : GRID : GRID : GRID : GRID : GRID
GRID : GRID : GRID : GRID : GRID : GRID
: : : : : : : : : : : : : : : : : : : : : : :
GRID : GRID : GRID : GRID : GRID : GRID
GRID : GRID : GRID : GRID : GRID : GRID
GRID : GRID : GRID : GRID : GRID : GRID
: : : : : : : : : : : : : : : : : : : : : : :
GRID : GRID : GRID : GRID : GRID : GRID
GRID : GRID : GRID : GRID : GRID : GRID
GRID : GRID : GRID : GRID : GRID : GRID
: : : : : : : : : : : : : : : : : : : : : : :
GRID : GRID : GRID : GRID : GRID : GRID
GRID : GRID : GRID : GRID : GRID : GRID
GRID : GRID : GRID : GRID : GRID : GRID
: : : : : : : : : : : : : : : : : : : : : : :
GRID : GRID : GRID : GRID : GRID : GRID
GRID : GRID : GRID : GRID : GRID : GRID
GRID : GRID : GRID : GRID : GRID : GRID
: : : : : : : : : : : : : : : : : : : : : : :
GRID : GRID : GRID : GRID : GRID : GRID
GRID : GRID : GRID : GRID : GRID : GRID
GRID : GRID : GRID : GRID : GRID : GRID

Letter to <u>Ettore Sottsass</u>
13 Apr.   2022

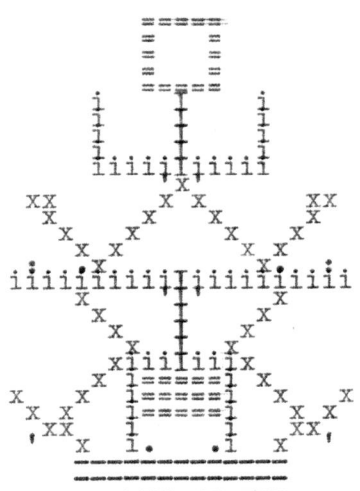

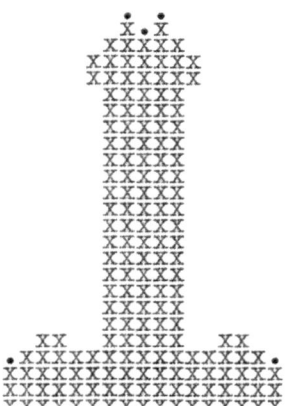

Letter to <u>El Lissitzky</u>
20 Apr.   2022

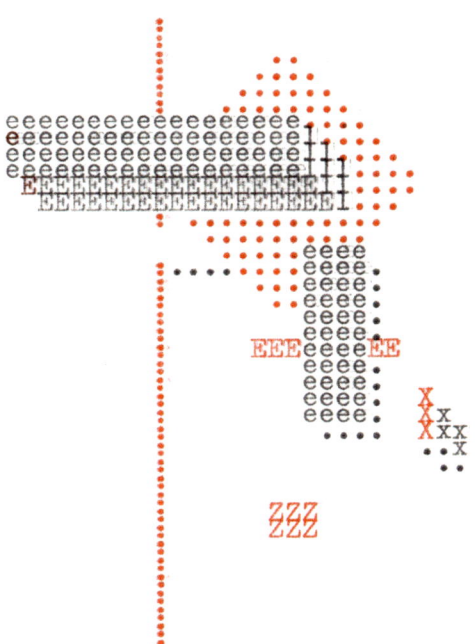

Letters to <u>Enzo Mari</u>
Jul. 31    2022

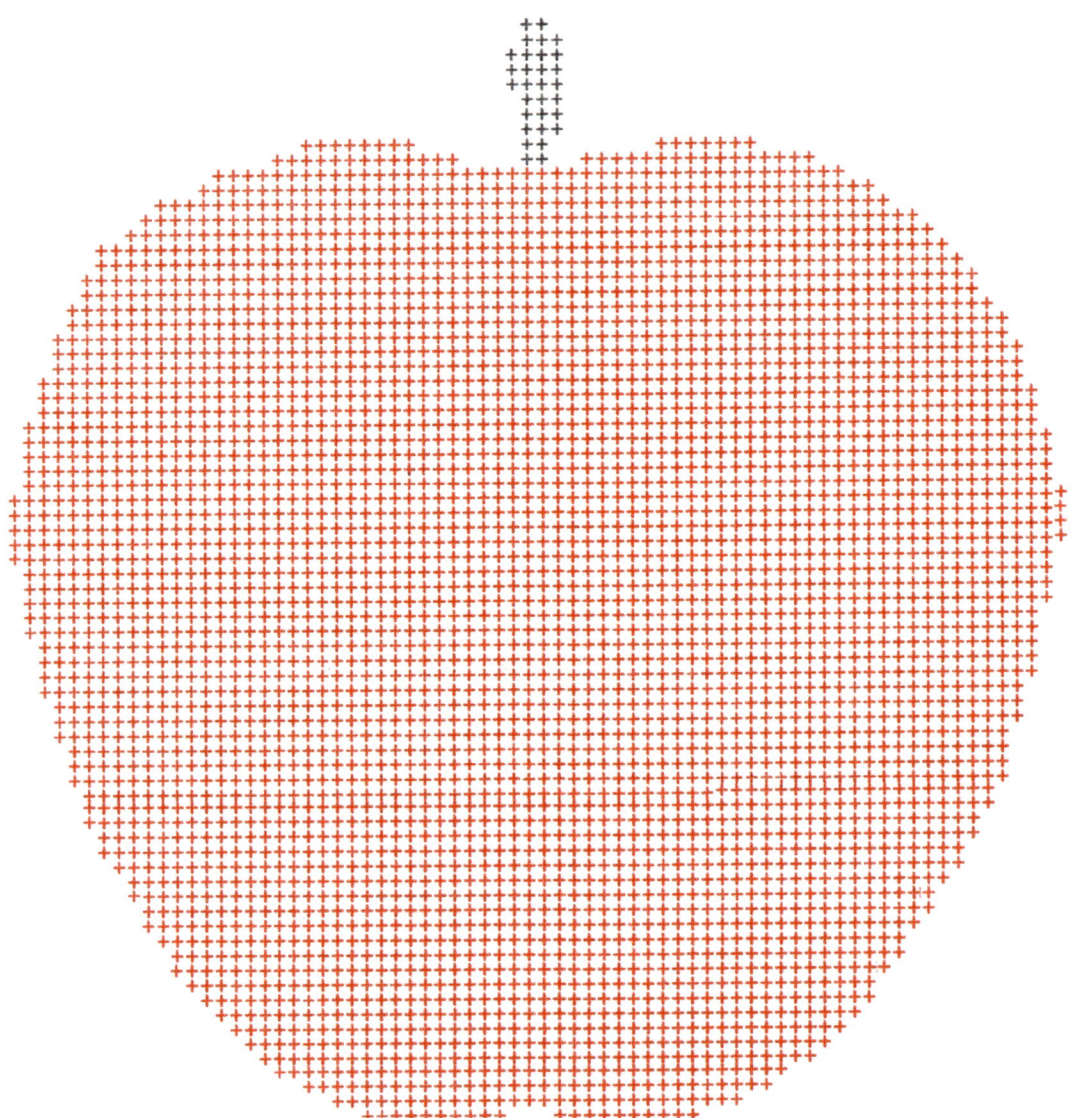

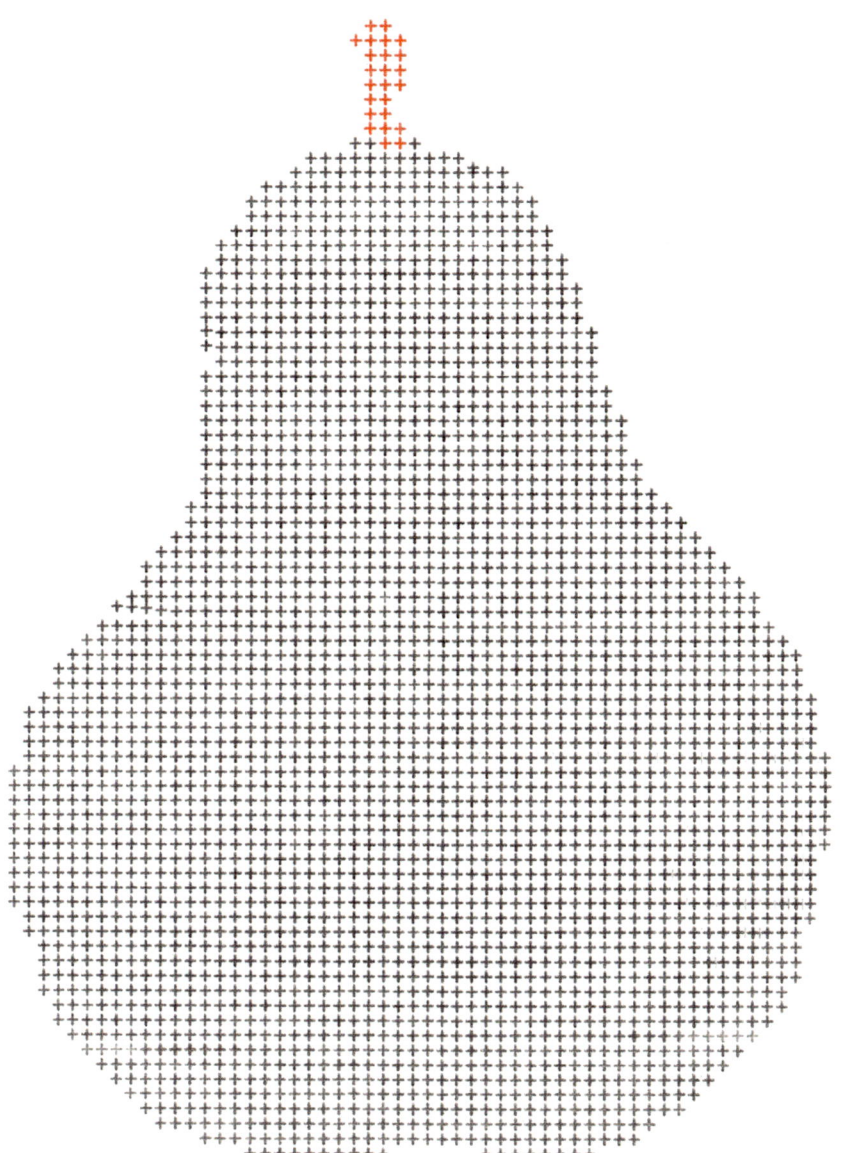

Letters to Park Seo-Bo
Sep. 14-21 2022

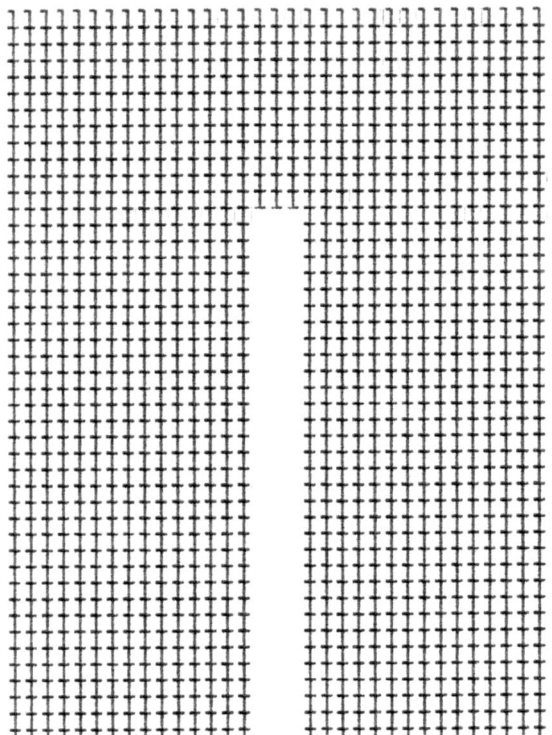

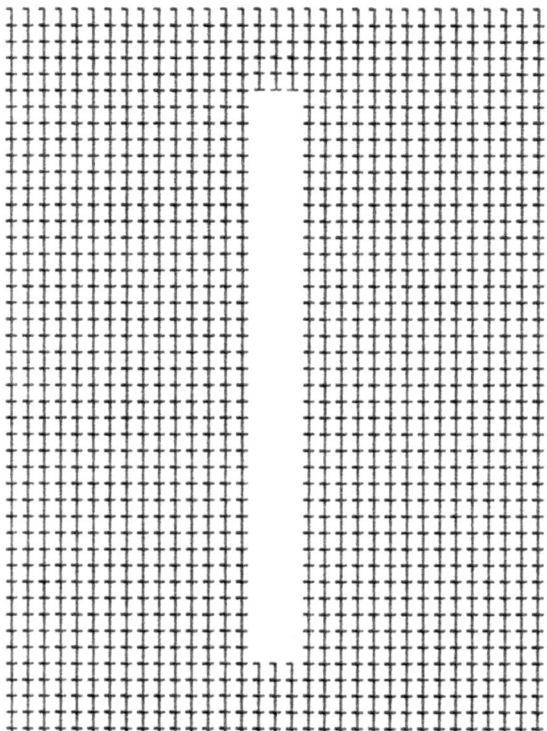

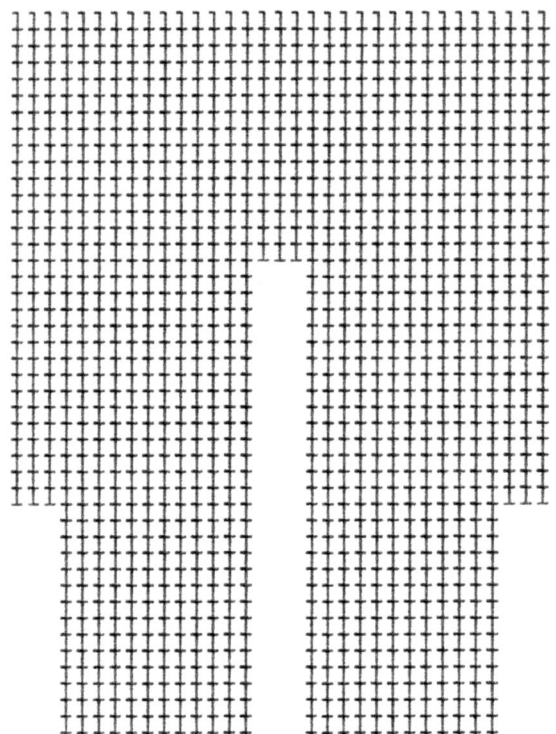

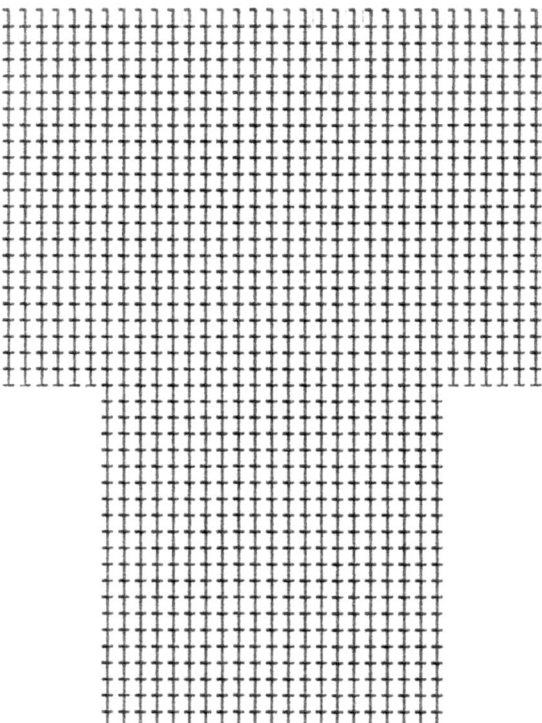

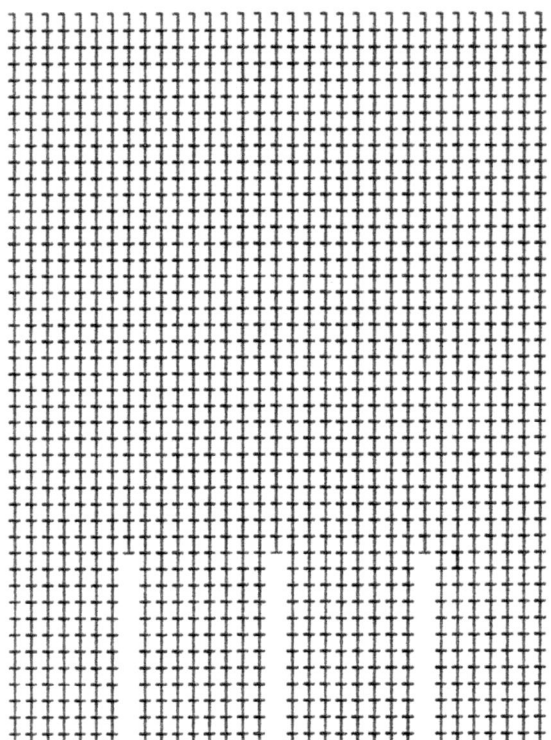

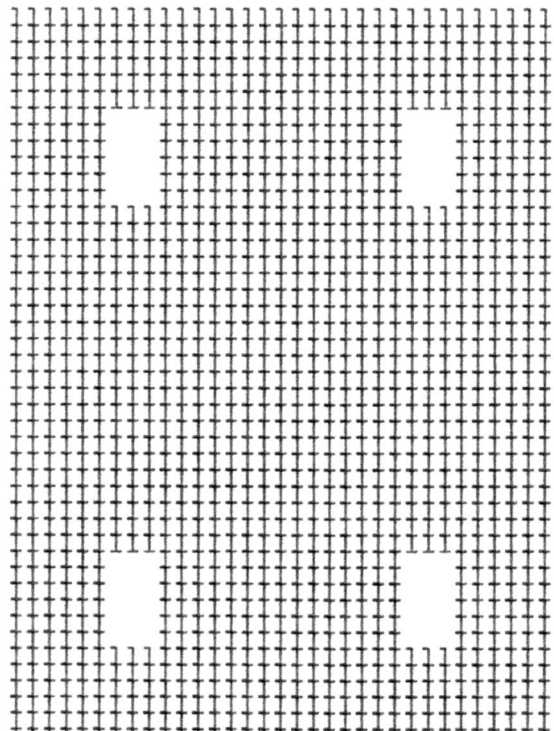

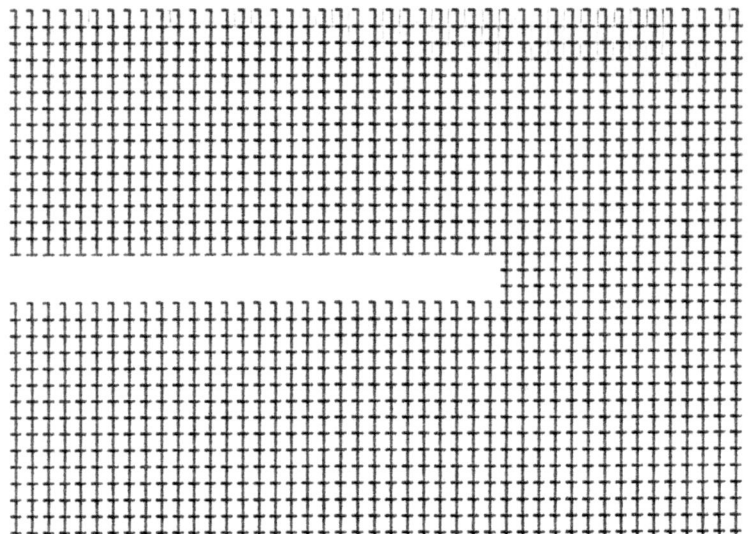

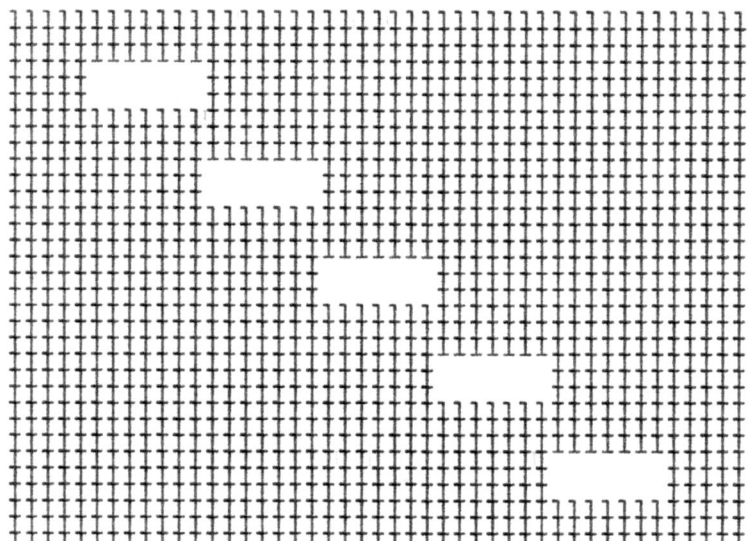

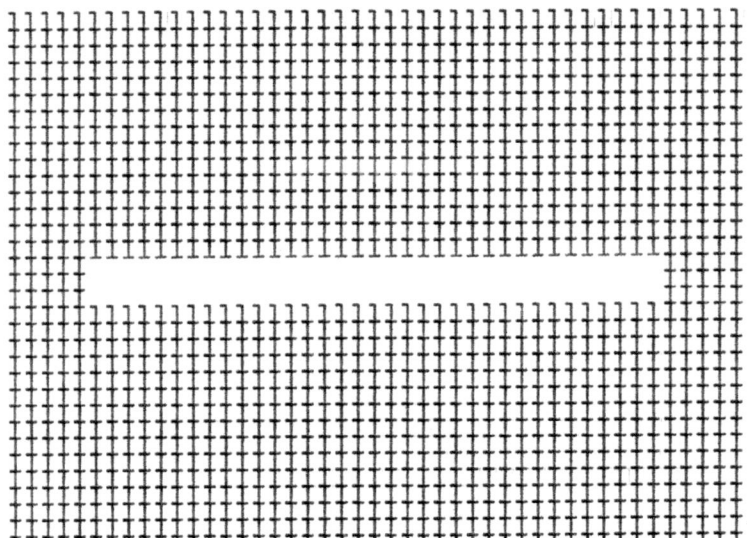

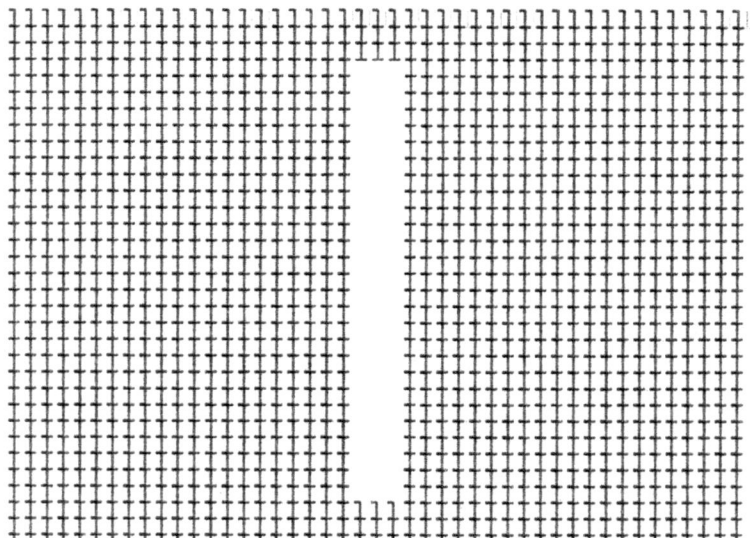

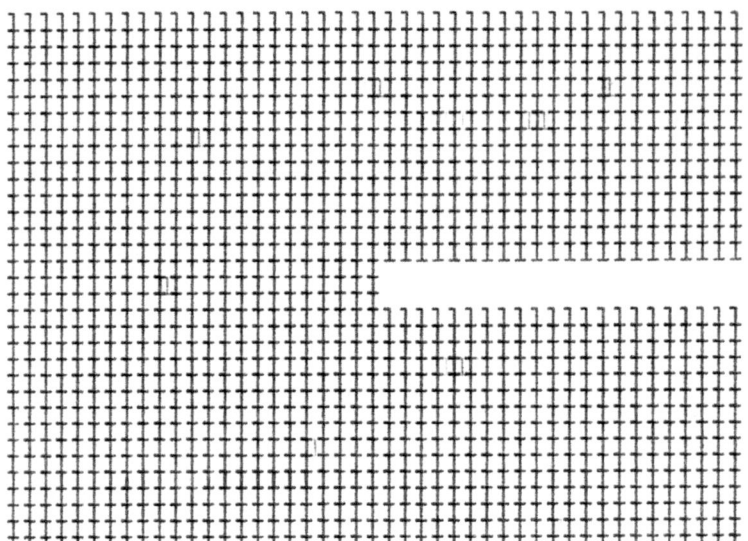

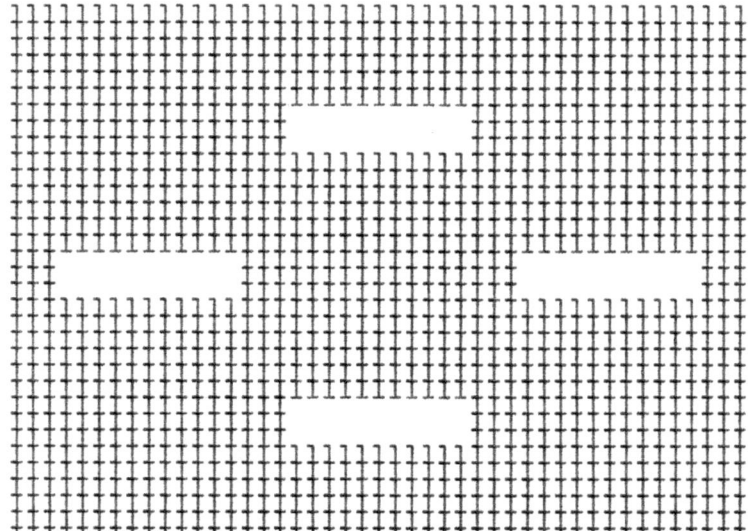

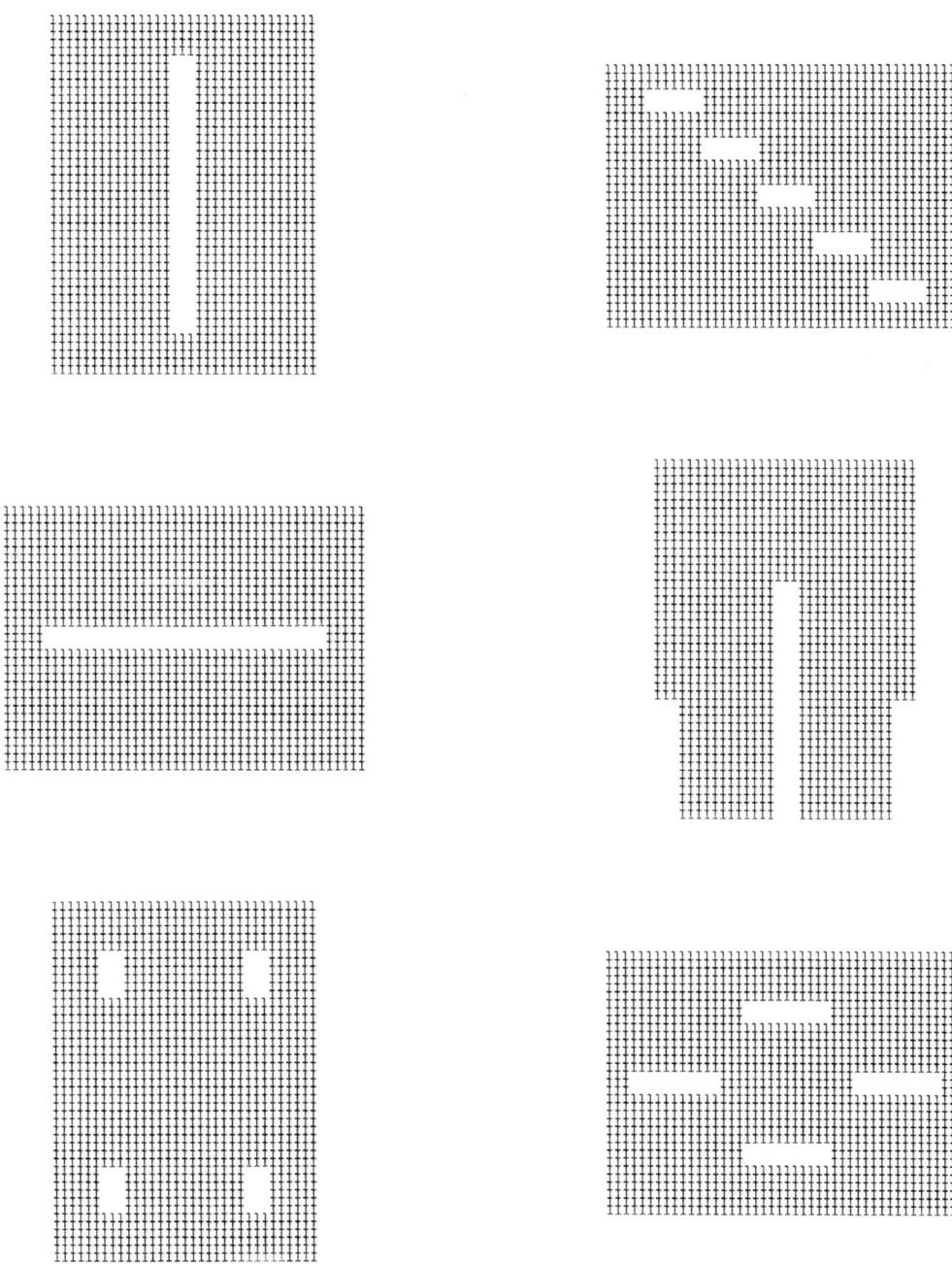

Letter to <u>IRAN</u>
Oct. 12    2022

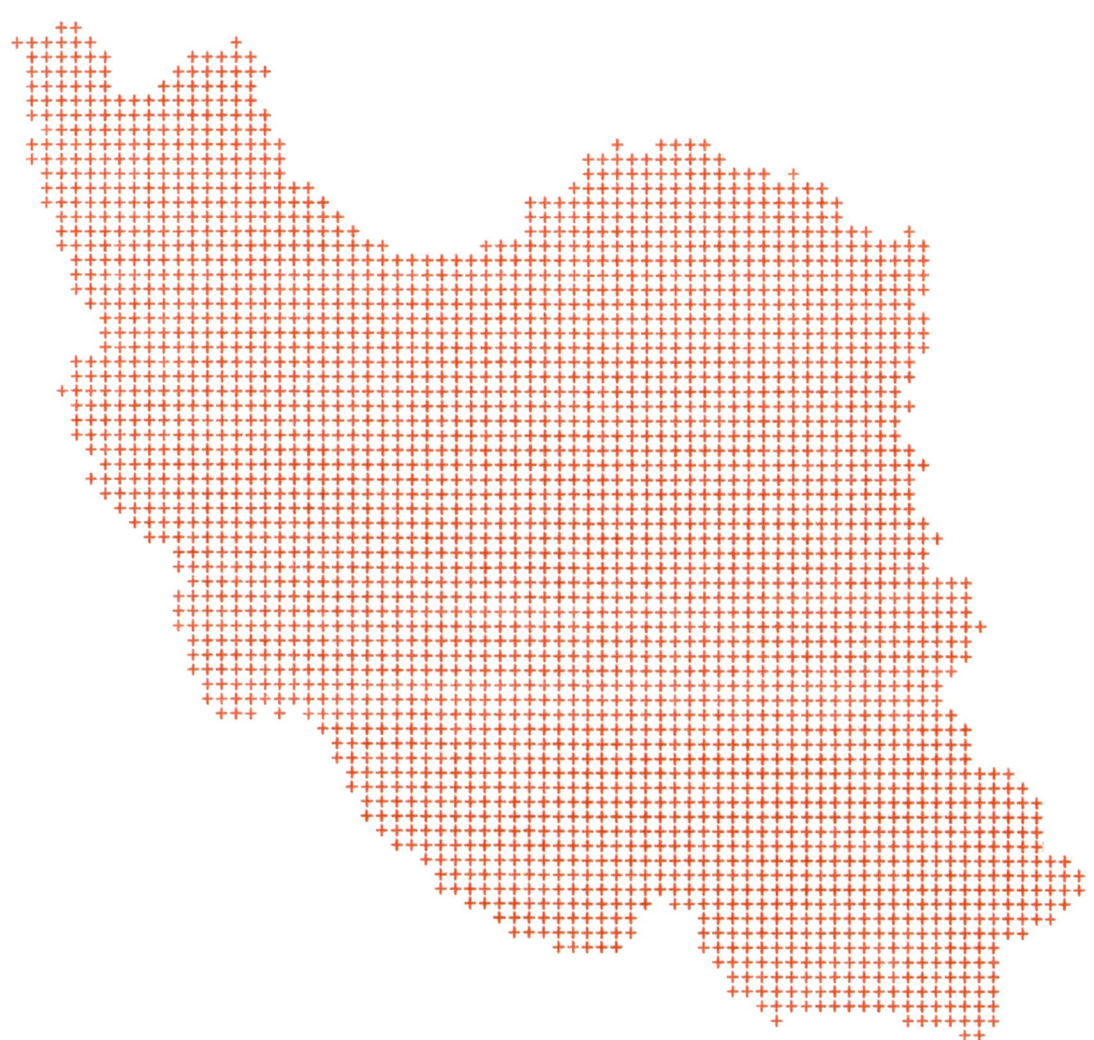

263

# ACKNOWLEDGMENTS

Thank you Ettore Sottsass & Perry King
Thank you Olivetti
Thank you Valentine

Thank you Massimo & Lella Vignelli
Thank you Vignelli Center for Design Studies
Thank you Josh Owen
Thank you R. Roger Remington

Thank you RIT Press
Thank you Marnie Soom
Thank you Alexandra Hoff

Thank you A B C D E F G H I J K L M N O P Q R S T U V W X Y Z :)

# INDEX

Reza Aliabadi (born 1974), known as RZLBD, is a Canadian artist and architect of Persian origin. He is the founder and principal of Atelier RZLBD, an art and architecture practice based in Toronto, named after a pseudonym he adapted that reflects his interest in abstraction and reduction. His repertoire of work extends to making arts, crafting objects, designing buildings, curating installations, and publishing a zine called rzlbdPOST.

His work has been distinguished with numerous accolades, exhibited in many venues, and celebrated in more than 100 print publications. In 2017, RZLBD was selected among the top emerging design talents in Canada. In the same year, the UK publisher Artifice released a monograph, *RZLBD Hopscotch*, that recognizes Aliabadi's selected built projects by collecting essays, project profiles, and annotated drawings. In 2020, Actar published a pocket-size manifesto, *The Empty Room*, in which Reza explores the idea of emptiness as the essence of architecture. His most recent book, *100 Rooms*, is a sequel to that title by the same publisher.

In 2023, he was appointed as the inaugural Vignelli Center Designer in Residence to begin the conceptualization, planning, and determining of the overall thematic direction of the RIT Outdoor Museum project.

**COLOPHON**

EDITOR
Alexandra Hoff

IDEATION AND CONCEPT
RZLBD

DESIGN AND PRODUCTION
Marnie Soom

TYPEFACE
Futura

PRINTING AND BINDING
More Vang

This book was made possible, in part,
through the generosity of More Vang.